Apollo Pilot

Outward Odyssey
A People's History of Spaceflight

Series editor
Colin Burgess

Apollo Pilot

The Memoir of Astronaut Donn Eisele

Donn Eisele

Edited and with a foreword by Francis French

Afterword by Susie Eisele Black

Historical overview by Amy Shira Teitel

UNIVERSITY OF NEBRASKA PRESS · LINCOLN & LONDON

All photographs are courtesy of
NASA.

Library of Congress Cataloging-in-
Publication Data
Names: Eisele, Donn, 1930–1987.
| French, Francis. | Eisele Black,
Susie. | Teitel, Amy Shira.
Title: Apollo pilot: the memoir
of astronaut Donn Eisele / Donn
Eisele; edited and with a foreword
by Francis French; afterword
by Susie Eisele Black; historical
overview by Amy Shira Teitel.
Description: Lincoln: University
of Nebraska Press, [2017] | Series:
Outward odyssey. A people's
history of spaceflight | Includes
bibliographical references and index.
Identifiers: LCCN 2016027504
ISBN 9780803262836
(cloth: alk. paper)
ISBN 9780803299528 (epub)
ISBN 9780803299535 (mobi)
ISBN 9780803299542 (pdf)
Subjects: LCSH: Eisele, Donn,
1930–1987. | Astronauts—United
States—Biography. | Project Apollo
(U.S.) | Apollo 7 (Spacecraft)
Classification: LCC TL789.85.E37 E37
2017 | DDC 629.450092 [B]—dc23
LC record available at https://
lccn.loc.gov/2016027504

Set in Adobe Garamond Pro
by Rachel Gould.

Contents

Illustrations

Foreword

Francis French

Donn Eisele was a curious conundrum. Voted most likely to succeed by his high school graduating class, he was seen as athletically gifted and academically very smart. Yet when interviewed during his Apollo years, his hometown colleagues said they never imagined Donn would do anything as adventurous as flying into space. He was a quiet, hard-working, well-liked guy. No one in Columbus, Ohio, seemed surprised that he had been a success in life. Nevertheless, a few had to look at old photos to confirm that they were talking about the right person. Donn Eisele didn't seem to leave a bad impression—rather, he breezed through many people's lives without leaving much of an impression at all.

Born in 1930 in Columbus, Ohio, the son of a newspaper printer, Eisele grew up in a very close, doting family. He hadn't planned to attend the Naval Academy, but he heard that his congressman was giving appointments on a competitive basis, and it might save his parents some money if the military paid his way through college. The day of the test, Eisele later admitted, was an excuse to be out of school. He felt he had only a slim chance of winning a spot in the prestigious academy, but to his surprise found the test easy.

Eisele had always been fascinated by flying, too, but didn't think he would ever pilot an aircraft. He hadn't imagined himself in the military as a youth, and he knew that learning to fly as a civilian was very expensive. He imagined a possible career in aeronautical engineering, as he was attracted to the technical side of aviation, but instead fell into an impressive flying career almost by accident.

Donn Eisele's story was one that intrigued me when I coauthored the space history book *In the Shadow of the Moon*. Eisele's fellow *Apollo 7* astronauts Wally Schirra and Walt Cunningham had become extremely helpful colleagues by then, and it would have been easy to write about *Apollo 7* from their viewpoint. Yet both had already written books about their space careers. Eisele, having passed away so young, twenty years before my book was published, was the untold story. He was the forgotten member of the crew, obscure enough that many space buffs were unsure how to spell his first name and pronounce his last name. Other astronauts didn't talk about him much either. Yet his story turned out to be a fascinating one. I was fortunate to be able to interview Wally Schirra, Gordon Cooper, Walt Cunningham, and Ed Mitchell—all the astronauts who trained with Eisele for space missions—along with many of his other colleagues, and as I did, the story grew ever more fascinating.

I learned, for instance, that fellow astronaut Tom Stafford seemed to have played a major role in all of Eisele's decisions once they both graduated from the Naval Academy and joined the air force. Stafford appears to have been the one to pull Eisele into both test pilot school and the astronaut corps. Once at NASA, Eisele came under the leadership of Wally Schirra, who had commanded Stafford's first spaceflight. Stafford served as backup commander for *Apollo 7*, and Eisele in turn served on the backup crew for *Apollo 10*, a flight to the moon that Stafford commanded. A person with an immense amount of respect and influence in the astronaut corps, Tom Stafford was an incredibly valuable ally for Eisele in his career leading up to *Apollo 7*.

Many who knew him well also recalled Eisele as somewhat forgetful and absent-minded in his personal life during his NASA training years. His wife Harriet sometimes had to run forgotten items out to him at the airstrip before he departed on another long round of testing or training elsewhere in the country. Yet with the untroubled demeanor also came an inner calm and patience that many noticed and appreciated.

An only child who lost both of his parents not long after he entered the space program, Donn was a self-admitted loner. Yet he had a goofy, lighthearted side that many recall fondly. Numerous stories from his contemporaries tell of him singing at social events, doing intentionally corny impersonations, or racing one of his children around the backyard while carrying another on his back. It seems he delighted in impersonating other entertainers when at parties, with a talent for mimicry that many enjoyed.

Selected for what was planned to be a relatively low-key mission—the second manned flight of Apollo, a mission that would largely repeat the first—Eisele was soon given a much weightier duty to perform. When the crew of the first Apollo mission died inside their spacecraft during ground testing in 1967, Eisele, along with Walt Cunningham and Wally Schirra, was tasked with preparing for the flight that would take America back into space. It was not just a case of flying after a major disaster—it had to be done soon, as time was running out for the Apollo program to achieve its ambition of landing astronauts on the moon by the end of the 1960s.

It was a difficult time for both Donn and Harriet. Both recounted at the time how reporters and people on the street continually referred to the *Apollo 1* fire when talking with them about Donn's upcoming flight. Like most people with military experience, Donn Eisele did not obsess about disaster, preferring instead to honor his lost colleagues by pressing on, learning the lessons of why they died while ensuring that such a tragedy was never repeated.

Having served on the prime crew for *Apollo 2*, then backup for *Apollo 1*, and now prime crew for the first manned flight, *Apollo 7*, Donn felt like he had been training with Wally and Walt forever by the time October 1968 rolled around and it was time to fly. For the very first time, three Americans would fly in space together. While NASA's earlier two-person Gemini flights had often paired an experienced astronaut with a rookie who had a similar background, for this mission the dynamics within the crew would be more complex. The crew was a diverse bunch, but highly motivated people such as astronauts knew how to work together well for the sake of the mission.

Schirra, one of the original Mercury astronauts chosen in 1959, had already declared that this would be his last flight, which gave him the freedom to be as opinionated as he wished. Many people noted that he seemed to have a different personality than in the prior decade, when he'd been considered jovial and wisecracking. The *Apollo 1* tragedy had changed his outlook. He was also increasingly feeling that the space business had devoured enough of his time and energy. Schirra felt that NASA was not the same organization that he had joined a decade earlier. He saw too many bureaucratic hurdles forming. He was ready to leave, but before doing so he brought a serious and demanding tone to the mission preparations. He resisted many changes to the spacecraft design, believing that individual engineers were not fully appreciating how one small change could affect many other systems in the complex spacecraft. Schirra was determined there would be no problems with this flight, and was equally resolute that preparations would go exactly his way. He was often blunt and ruffled many feathers.

It was an understandable response given the deaths of the prior crew, but Eisele noted that many in the Apollo team felt put out by the single-mindedness with which Schirra got his way. Schirra was a naval aviator, and he felt it was important to remind people that naval commanders were in charge of their vessels. Mission Control could advise and suggest, but ultimately he would decide. He felt that the flight controllers, generally younger than him, had much less experience than he did with complex engineering systems. Eisele and Cunningham, subordinate to their commander, had little choice but to follow his lead. Cunningham later reflected that, with a strong personality such as Schirra in command, it was not surprising that Eisele was heavily influenced by him.

Eisele's easygoing style was an asset, as he could breeze through clashes and disagreements easier than most. He often became the calming referee between pilots and managers. However, he often found himself agreeing with some of Schirra's complaints, and later reflected that some officials soon wrote the crew off as troublemakers for raising awkward questions. Despite their differing personalities, the crew seemed to bond well; one person noted that by the time of the flight, Donn's laugh was identical to Wally's.

Walt Cunningham, unlike Schirra and Eisele, had never been a test pilot, but instead brought an impressive science background to the crew. After flying fighter jets in the Marine Corps, he gained a doctorate in physics from UCLA while also working for the RAND Corporation on space-related projects. Always a candid, opinionated person, Cunningham later reflected that his personality did not help his career once he joined NASA and hoped for a spaceflight assignment. He was too obstinate, he admitted, to play that game well. Deke Slayton, who made the crew selections, considered him more of a scientist than an aviator, something that also did not work in his favor.

Schirra was impressed by Cunningham's thorough knowledge of the spacecraft systems, and Cunningham had great respect for his commander in return—especially his innate flying skills. Yet he also chafed against

Schirra's insistence on being in charge even when, as it seemed to Cunningham, there were many occasions when no one cared.

Despite serving on the *Apollo 10* backup crew, Donn Eisele never flew in space again after *Apollo 7*. Opinions vary on why. Some say that disagreements with Mission Control during the flight made NASA officials wary of flying any of the crew again. There were seemingly innocuous items such as Schirra not wishing to test the in-flight television circuit until he was ready, and choosing not to wear a space helmet on reentry out of concern that he would not be able to clear his ears with a bad head cold and changing cabin pressure. The crew devised a system to secure their heads in their couches without helmets, and they successfully tested the television once Schirra was satisfied with the circuit test. Nevertheless, these small disagreements seem to have left many on the ground with bad feelings about the crew.

Others say that Donn's decision to divorce Harriet and remarry very shortly afterward broke an unspoken code about the all-American, apple-pie image that astronauts were supposed to portray. By the time of his divorce in the late 1960s, much of America had moved on from such issues. But as the first astronaut to divorce, Eisele was a test case that did not go well.

It is unfortunate that these perceptions now cloud the outstanding work that Donn Eisele performed in space. As a pilot on the first test flight of NASA's most complex spacecraft at that time, Eisele had to test one of its most vital elements—the guidance and navigation system that would allow the astronauts to know where they were, and how to get home. The next mission would use this system to navigate all the way to the moon and back. Eisele not only thoroughly tested it, he also uncovered numerous places where procedures could be improved. Without this work, missions such as *Apollo 11* could not have flown. Wally Schirra certainly seemed pleased with his colleague's work and the way Eisele double-checked him in orbit, explaining in the postflight technical debriefings that "this is the way two aviators or pilots work. You learn to work together in a pilot/copilot relationship, and I think Donn and I have spent enough time on these systems together where we could overlap, and that was good."

Placed in a management position within NASA far away from the action in Houston, Donn Eisele retired from NASA and the air force in 1972. His second marriage, to Susie, was a very happy and successful one that lasted until the day he died, at the relatively young age of fifty-seven. While other astronauts of the Apollo era have remained in the public consciousness through public appearances and writing memoirs, Donn Eisele's name faded into relative obscurity.

Some time after the publication of *In the Shadow of the Moon*, I was a guest at the home of Susie Eisele Black and her husband, Bob, in Florida. Susie encouraged me to look through a closet full of boxes containing many items that belonged to her late husband, including numerous objects he had used in space on *Apollo 7*. While looking through the files, I came across a stack of translucent onionskin paper. Leafing through the pages, I realized I had stumbled across a number of typewritten drafts by Donn of an unpublished memoir.

There were at least five different drafts, written in differing styles. Some stopped abruptly in mid-sentence, and in others it was clear by the page numbers that parts were forever missing. A few had faded so much that the only way to read them was to scan them and, like a forensic detective, create a negative image of the page so that individual words could be carefully teased back from oblivion. In reading it all, however, it was clear that there was enough remaining to construct a memoir of Donn Eisele's NASA years up to and including his *Apollo 7* flight.

It is difficult to say from the drafts alone exactly when Eisele wrote them. Little hints about the number of years since Apollo events suggest much was probably written within the 1973–76 time frame. Susie recalls Donn working on drafts in 1971–72, and beginning again in 1974 after returning from serving in Thailand. This would explain not only the freshness of many of his recollections but also much of the apparent anger Eisele still felt toward a number of people he had worked with. These were years when Donn Eisele had just left NASA, believing he had been frozen out of a second spaceflight, and he clearly felt he had some scores to settle on paper. While he also gives a lot of praise, he is unsparing when it comes to criticizing some managers and fellow astronauts. He also does not hold back when it comes to the illicit activities of his colleagues away from home.

Three things should be noted when reading the drafts. It can never be known what final form Donn Eisele would have settled on. Pages are missing, and he may have chosen to add to, tone down, or rewrite some of his personal observations in subsequent drafts. The meaning of some words, such as "retarded" to describe a much-loved child with Down syndrome, has changed over the decades. At the time, that was a term still frequently used by doctors. Susie also explained to me that "Donn and Wally used to say 'Oh, sob' all the time. It was a standard saying of the two of them. It means whining, or crying, just like 'boohoo.'"

It should also be noted that the in-flight conversations quoted do not match the actual flight transcripts. Rather, I am assuming that Eisele is portraying the atmosphere of the conversations during *Apollo 7*, and his general impressions of the mood of the flight.

The force and candor of some of his opinions and observations made me reconsider whether to work on his drafts for publication. However, I decided I needed to set those concerns against a wider picture. The Apollo program will forever be one of the greatest achievements of humanity. There are those who say that, in future centuries, it may be one of the only things the twentieth century is remembered for. There can also only ever be one first Apollo flight: and on that first Command Module spacecraft, one Command Module pilot. I decided that it was not really up to me. If historians stumbled across, say, a sixteenth-century diary of one of the voyagers accompanying Ferdinand Magellan on the first circumnavigation of the earth, what might they do? I decided the need to share for the sake of history would outweigh concerns about the specific content.

Besides, Eisele's candid account reveals his views of disagreements in management style and mission command, as well as the personal lives of the astronauts, that other histories gloss over. Not everyone involved in Apollo will agree with Donn Eisele's viewpoints. In fact, many will not. But that does not make his thoughts any less interesting to read. As Donn Eisele himself states in the following chapters, "We were insolent, highhanded, and Machiavellian at times. Call it paranoia, call it smart—it got the job done. We had a great flight. Anything less might have meant the end of the program. And I'd rather be called a shithead and live through it than have everybody remember what a nice guy I was."

(And just so you know—it is pronounced "Eyes-Lee" . . .)

Apollo Pilot

1. Launch Morning

The sun rose high over blue Florida waters on a bright October morning. Palm trees swayed and fluttered in the brisk ocean breeze. Launch day was clear, bright, cloudless and windy.

There was a lot of wildlife around the Cape. On the beach and in the palmetto marshes of the Cape, I knew all the creatures were beginning to stir. I imagined toads sleeping under a rock at the foot of a water tower, dreaming of flies, mosquitoes, and whatever else hungry toads like to eat. In nearby ponds and canals, alligators would be raising their long pointed snouts out of the water, giving a contented alligator grunt and crawling onto the banks. The warm sun would feel good on their green leathery backs, and they would be switching their tails lazily back and forth. Crabs would be peeking out of their beach houses—holes in the sand—and looking about for a tasty breakfast morsel.

I don't know if it was cool out there or not. I couldn't tell with that big lumpy pressure suit on. Fact is, it was too windy: straight off the ocean at twenty-plus knots. Eighteen knots was our safe limit, based on the need for the spacecraft to land in the water in case of a low altitude or launch pad abort. An impact on dry land could have caused severe injury to us. With the onshore wind like that and a low altitude abort, we could have landed over on Merritt Island someplace and got hurt.

There wasn't any excuse, really. The management was supposed to remain objective and make rational, unemotional judgments in the interest of mission success and crew safety. I remember one time some years before I got on a flight crew when I was expressing to Apollo program manager Joe Shea my dismay over the miserly amount of attitude control propellant spelled out in the Apollo design. He said to me, "Donn, you just worry about getting ready to fly and let us worry about the spacecraft design. We'll take care of you. Don't worry." He took care of us, all right. Ask Gus, Roger, and Ed of the *Apollo 1* crew. Oops, sorry, they're not around anymore. Sorry about that test, fellows. But we had to go, go, go, to meet the launch schedule. And by the way, after Shea left we got an increase of 60 percent in the attitude fuel for all but the first spacecraft.

Meanwhile, back to launch day. Wally Schirra, Walt Cunningham, and I got up, got a fast physical, then had a great breakfast of steak and eggs. There were several visitors and guests there in the dining room that morning. Funny, I can't even remember who they were. George Low, I guess, and Kenny Kleinknecht, and John Healey, and maybe George Mueller or Sam Phillips. There were three or four photographers snapping away at us. Maybe it was only one guy, I don't know, but it seemed like more. I read the morning paper until it was time to go. I wonder if old Walt still carries a newspaper around with him everywhere? He'd never go anyplace without that damn paper tucked under his arm.

We went to the suit room to suit up. Everyone was "up" for the occasion and in good spirits, but one of the medical technicians was nervous as hell. A few days before, Wally had really chewed his ass because one of Walt's sensor leads was too long. It was really a trivial matter, and Walt didn't really care that much, and anyway it wasn't the tech's fault. He had nothing to do with the harness design. But then, you know Wally. Always the prima donna. He had a hard-on for the medics, too. I guess we all did to some extent. If you didn't offer some resistance to them, they'd have draped us from head to toe with sensors, leads, signal conditioners, and pins in our scalps.

We got our suits on and checked out with time to spare. At the appointed minute, we left the suit room and walked to the elevator. The corridor was packed with secretaries, technicians, and other workers in the building. I remember the festive mood; hundreds of people turned out to see us leave the operations building. They were lined up along the hallways and the walkway to the transfer van, cheering and waving and wishing us well. Smiling, they shouted encouragement and good luck. It was a very happy occasion, and a touching one for the three of us.

We got off the elevator at ground level and found the same reception on our stroll to the transfer van, which was to take us out to Pad 34 for launch. There were people all along the driveway, in the parking lot, and along the main road in front of the Mission Support Building.

We all piled into the van. There were the three of us plus our boss, Deke Slayton, and three suit technicians, the driver, and the security officer. Wally, Walt, and I were all cooped up in our suits and carried our own portable oxygen packs. There was a communications system in the van that we could plug into so we could all talk with each other. I remember telling Deke to take care of things on the beach for us. Deke responded with an ill-at-ease smile. The suit techs, the driver, and the security officer were listening to our conversation. Deke was nervous about anyone outside of our group knowing or hearing about our little romantic goings-on in Cocoa Beach.

The van had big windows in it. As we approached the causeway, I could see out across the broad flat stretch of Banana River water and grasslands to the launch pad. There stood that beautiful white rocket, spewing white fumes of oxygen boil-off. When we got to the gate, Deke got off and went into the blockhouse. Then the van took us to the elevator at the base of the gantry. It was eerie and desolate out there. Normally when we went out to the pad there were a lot of people. Launch day was different.

Wally and Walt went up first with their suit techs, because the little passageway you had to cross to get to the spacecraft wasn't big enough for all of us. I had about ten minutes to kill until someone came down so I could go up.

I got out of the van to get a good look at our rocket. It was spectacular. There I stood in my lumpy white suit with the clear bubble helmet, lugging my portable oxygen supply, staring straight up at the monster. I walked around the base of the rocket, looking up at it like a country boy getting his first view of a big city skyscraper. Of course I had seen it before, but not like this—the rocket glistening in the bright morning sun, the launch pad deserted, liquid oxygen boiling off white vapors—I felt awed, dwarfed by this huge vehicle and the awareness that soon it would carry me to orbit. I remember thinking, "It's like launching the Washington Monument." A numbing experience—but it was good to know that after all these months and years of preparation we were finally going to launch this beauty.

When the ten minutes expired, my suit tech, Keith, and I went up the elevator. At the top we had to cross a thirty-foot catwalk on the access arm to get to the white room that enclosed the spacecraft hatch. The gantry swayed noticeably in the twenty-knot breeze, and the access arm, cantilevered out from it, felt pretty flimsy as it lurched and vibrated. Our favorite pad leader, Guenter Wendt, was in charge inside the white room and had the whole operation well under control.

It didn't take long to get me strapped in. Then they closed and locked the hatch. We checked the latches on the inside. Guenter and his crew began disassembling the white room. Just before they left, Guenter took one last look at us through the hatch window. I gave him a thumbs-up. He smiled and waved, then disappeared. A few minutes later the white room and access arm moved back away from the spacecraft. Guenter was the last person I saw before liftoff and that was the last time I ever saw him. Ironic, in a way.

We had nearly two hours to wait before liftoff. It seemed like an eternity. We had a few things to do during some of the pre-launch checks, but mostly it was just lying there on our backs waiting for the time to run out.

The sun beat down on the concrete launch pad and warmed the backs of the weary men who had worked there all through the night. Now they were rushing to finish up the last-minute chores before scurrying off in their cars and trucks. Towering above the launch pad stood our giant Saturn rocket, gleaming white in the bright sun and spouting white clouds of vapor. At the top of the rocket, we lay tucked away inside our spacecraft, waiting quietly while the last few minutes until liftoff ticked away.

This was it. The moment I had been waiting for through days, months, years of preparation. I found myself thinking: Donn Eisele, air force pilot, member of the Apollo space program, astronaut, you are about to rocket into space on the first Apollo mission. I looked at the panel of instruments in front of me and at my crewmates. Wally Schirra on my left and Walt Cunningham on my right, all three of us strapped tightly to our seats and lying flat on our backs. We were relaxed and confident as we awaited the final minutes of the countdown. I thought about the procedures during launch, my duties in orbit, about all the things I'd be doing in space for the next eleven days. And sometimes when there was a lull in the count my mind wandered off to other things, like the ancient Greeks and their stories of Daedalus who flew on wings of wax and feathers, and his son Icarus who fell into the sea when he flew too close to the sun and his wings melted.

Even in those ancient times men dreamed of flying, yet were fearful of it. I recalled *Buck Rogers* and *Flash Gordon*, those comic strips that I never read as a boy because they seemed too far-fetched, too preposterous. But this wasn't a comic strip happening—this flight I was about to make was real. No make-believe adventure, no wax-and-feathers fantasy. This was the first Apollo shot, the spaceship that would eventually go to the moon. And because it was real, and here and now, it was far more exciting, more fantastic than anything I ever saw in the Sunday comics.

"*Apollo 7*, do you read?" crackled a voice in our earphones.

"We read you loud and clear," answered Wally. "The crew is 'go' for launch."

"TEN, NINE, EIGHT . . . ," boomed a heavy voice counting down the last seconds to launch. ". . . THREE, TWO, ONE . . ."

2. Beginnings

I find myself thinking back, trying to remember where it all began. But who can ever pinpoint exact beginnings? I can remember, at the age of two or three, running outside—or getting someone to take me out whenever a plane flew overhead. I guess I was always fascinated by airplanes, and was there ever a time when I didn't want to be a pilot? Certainly through all my years at school, back home in Columbus, Ohio, I knew that was what I would like to do.

When I graduated from high school I enrolled in the Naval Academy at Annapolis, and out of the Academy I went right into air force pilot training. I flew jet fighters for several years, then returned to college to study astronautics—the science of spaceflight. The studies were interesting and so was my duty afterward, in technical work. But I yearned to fly again. I missed the whine and smell and roar of jet engines. The wheeling, soaring freedom of high flight, turning and weaving, playing tag with great towering pillars of boiling white clouds. The solid feel of g-forces in a tight turn or pullout from a dive. So I returned to the cockpit, this time as a test pilot, to blend flying with my training as an engineer.

In 1962 Charlie Bassett, Ted Freeman, and I were in test pilot school together. There were sixteen in the class, and in proper military fashion we arranged ourselves in alphabetical order. It happened that Charlie sat directly in front of me, and Ted sat immediately to my right. It also happened that the three of us were the top three students in the class, and were the three who wound up later going to NASA as astronauts—but not before a false start or two.

About halfway through the course, in April or May, NASA announced a second round of astronaut selections—the so-called Gemini astronauts. One of the qualifications was that applicants had to be practicing test pilots or have graduated from a test pilot school. Charlie, Ted, and I tried to apply, reasoning that we would have completed the course by the time final selections were made. But we reckoned without the Edwards Air Force Base Astronaut Screening Board—or whatever title it went by (there may not have been a board as such, but in effect there was)—which decreed that we were ineligible on account of not having graduated yet from test pilot school and until we had, presumably and theoretically there was always the chance we wouldn't. High-handed snobbery of the most callous sort, we thought. We were all doing well and there were no doubts of our completing the program with honors—barring some calamity that might wipe us out of flying altogether.

The pre-screening of astronaut applicants at Edwards by the local honchos was required by neither the air force nor NASA. The principal reason, we were told, was to assure that all applicants were fully qualified, so that none would bounce back from air force headquarters and thus make Edwards look bad. The real reason was to ensure as far as possible that the chosen fair-haired few would have the least competition and therefore the best chance of being passed on to NASA by air force headquarters.

As it turned out, that's about what happened. Of the nine men finally selected by NASA, four were air force, of which three came from Edwards: Jim McDivitt, Frank Borman, and Tom Stafford. McDivitt and Borman were among the heavy favorites. (Curiously, the other darlings of the Edwards ruling clique didn't get past air force screening.) Stafford was an instructor at the test pilot school at the time, a post not necessarily high on the Edwards pecking order, compared to flying the more exotic aircraft like the X-15, the U-2, or the latest jet fighter prototype. When Tom first got wind of the screening ploys, he raced over to wing headquarters and raised enough hell with the colonels on the senior staff to get assurances that his application would be forwarded with no qualifications or adverse commentary.

Stafford had a point. He had stood first in his class at test pilot school and had been instrumental, in his instructor role, in revamping and streamlining the course material and instructing methods. He was one of the most skillful pilots at the test center, and Edwards management would have been hard pressed to defend anything less than full approval of his application for astronaut training.

For Eisele, Bassett, and Freeman, the story was different. Our applications hit a stone wall at Edwards and bounced back in our faces with curt insinuations that we were categorically unfit for the exalted role of astronaut—a prejudicial and unwarranted assumption, we felt, since the space agency presumably knew better than anyone else who was fit and who wasn't.

Charlie Bassett, ever the nice guy and non-wave-maker, dropped out at that point. But not boat-rocker Freeman and bullhead Eisele. We fired our applications directly to the NASA space center in Houston. We expected to get our wrists slapped, but at least NASA would know we existed even if they couldn't pick us (unlikely without air force sanction). And next time, if there ever were a next time, we might have a better chance. But nothing much happened. Several weeks later Ted and I got a polite brush-off letter from Warren North at the Houston center thanking us for our interest but stating they couldn't process our applications since they didn't come through channels—and better luck next time.

I dismissed my chances. It had been about three years between the selection of the first and second astronaut groups, and I figured I'd be too old by the time NASA got around to a third. I guessed they would start reducing the upper age limit, going for younger candidates.

We finished our test pilot training in August. Charlie Bassett walked off with all the marbles, standing first overall and in academics as well. Ted Freeman was second and I ran a close third. In the scramble for assignments, I secured a billet as a fighter test pilot at Kirtland Air Force Base in Albuquerque, New Mexico. But I was told to plan on staying at Edwards another six or eight months to attend the first class of the new Space Research Pilots program. Later this course was incorporated into the regular training curriculum but at first it was separate, and made a big deal of.

Charlie and Ted emerged among the handpicked dozen or so primary candidates as I slipped to alternate status. I felt like the proverbial butter-fingered bridesmaid. There was scant chance I'd get to attend the course, but I was constrained to hang around Edwards for two or three months on the off chance that some of the primary guys would flunk their physicals or otherwise get shot down.

Meanwhile, my juicy flying job at Kirtland Air Base in Albuquerque got shaky. I started getting calls from other bases: El Centro in the Imperial Valley near Mexico, to fly cargo planes for parachute drop tests; Eglin, in Florida, to work on jungle warfare in old propeller-driven trainers; and other places to do a variety of jobs, some of them not even flying assignments. Finally I flew to Washington and managed to shake loose the orders sending me to Kirtland. The space pilot course began with all the primary selectees in attendance, and I left immediately for New Mexico with my family. Just before we left Edwards, Buck Buchanan, the officer in charge of the space pilot school, told me another course would start in about six months and he felt sure I could make it if I applied. I told him if I were all that hot a prospect he should have put me in the first class while I was still there at Edwards instead of dragging in a bunch of other guys from all over the country while I hung by my thumbs to see whether they would all make it, then send me elsewhere only to drag me back six months later. I was beginning to feel like a yo-yo on a string. He said I had a point, but air force headquarters had gotten into the act of selecting candidates and he didn't have control of it. I never did find out if that was true, but his story sounded like a cop-out to me. At that point it didn't matter anymore, since I had had my fill of formal training and was eager to get on with my first assignment as a test pilot.

We arrived in Albuquerque and found a house to rent in the northeast section near the foot of majestic Sandia Mountain. We were several miles from it but the mountain is so steep and high, and the air so clear there, that it appeared to be at our doorstep. Melinda and Donn, my two older children, settled into the routine of their new school, down the street about two blocks. My wife, Harriet, busied herself with the prosaic chores of housekeeping. Matt, our little retarded fellow, played, giggled, bawled, and got into minor mischief (he planted his foot in a bucket of paint while I was painting the walls) and made us all laugh—and cry.

I threw myself into the business of learning the ropes in the new assignment. After the customary "new guy" skepticism subsided, I was allowed to acquaint myself with the F-104 Starfighter—a long needle-like airplane with little stubs for wings, a great high T-shaped tail, and an enormously powerful engine. It was fast, very fast, and deceptively easy to fly. But the 104 could get you into trouble quickly if you didn't watch what you were doing. I also flew occasionally in the F-100, the first (barely) supersonic fighter, and the ubiquitous T-33 jet trainer that I had flown almost continuously since pilot training days.

Kirtland was a peculiar place for a flight test organization. The com-

manding general was an old man with only three thousand hours of flying time to show for his thirty years in the air force. And most of that was
in old propeller-driven transports on routine administrative and training
flights. One wondered why he bothered to fly at all. His understanding of
test work was abysmally deficient and his approach to flying seemed to be,
the less of it, the better. Ideally if no one flew there would be zero accidents
and therefore a perfect safety record. But he was a pleasant and engaging
old gent, well-liked and respected by his people, and the Special Weapons
Center seemed to function with efficiency under his direction.

In flight operations our sole excuse for existence was to serve the flight
test needs of the Atomic Energy Commission at nearby Sandia Army Base.
Most of the test flights consisted of dropping bomb-like objects to test the
fuses and other inner workings of "special weapons," the air force euphe-
mism for nuclear bombs. We also took on other odd jobs in the way of test
flying whenever they came our way. But mostly we flew around on routine training flights—fun in a way, but not especially stimulating. There
was no dearth of funds or flying hour allocations, and we bored holes in
the skies all over New Mexico and southern Colorado. Several times I saw
large herds of elk, two or three hundred of them, wandering across the high
slopes near the Colorado border.

Early in 1963 I acquired an old B-57 twin jet bomber that had been res-
urrected out of the "boneyard" in Tucson, Arizona, the burial ground for
old air force planes. This particular craft had a fifteen-foot-long appendage stuck on the front end of the fuselage. At one time the proboscis had
carried instruments for testing some parts of the guidance system of the
Bomarc missile. The task of flying the old turkey fell to me, largely on the
strength of a few hours' flight time I had gotten in B-57s at Edwards—but
also because nobody else wanted to do it. We had two programs to carry
out with the B-57, both having to do with developing air-launched rockets
for sampling the atmosphere. I got the job of project officer as well as chief
pilot for both of them—good experience, but I resented the time taken
away from flying the F-104s.

In February of 1963, when I had been at Kirtland Air Base three months,
a message came in asking if I or John Sexton, another recent graduate of
Edwards, wanted to return there to attend the second class of the space pilot
course. John wasn't interested, and I declined because we had just gotten set-

tled in Albuquerque and it didn't seem worth the effort. Besides, I really dug New Mexico and the flying at Kirtland. There was no guarantee I'd get the same post, or another anywhere near as nice, if I went off to school again.

When public school let out in June, Harriet and I packed up the kids and went on leave back to Ohio to see our parents. It seems that all our vacations, through all the years I was married to her, were spent in Ohio. We both were very closely tied to parents, family, and hometown friends. Neither of us really ever cut the umbilical cord. We talked a lot about doing something different on the next vacation, but each time the opportunity arose we succumbed to our homesick yearnings and opted instead for returning to the womb. The summer of '63 was no exception.

My parents lived in a small brick home in the western suburbs of Columbus, Ohio. They had moved there a few years earlier from a larger home after my grandfather died. He had lived with them since 1930. The new house eminently suited their needs. It was compact, convenient, and efficient. When I arrived with brood in tow, the house fairly bulged at the seams. After a few days my parents, especially Mom, would get tense and start haranguing.

A day or two after we arrived in Columbus, I noticed a small article in the evening paper concerning the selection of a new group of astronauts. According to the article, NASA was soliciting applications from civilian rather than military pilots. I felt disappointed at being excluded a priori but rationalized that it didn't really matter because I liked my situation at Albuquerque. And anyway, I wouldn't have much chance getting past the air force screening since I had turned down the offer to attend the space pilot course at Edwards.

A few days later on a pleasant sunny afternoon (the weather seldom gets stuffy in central Ohio until July or August), we were sitting on the back patio. (Did we ever do anything there except sit on the patio or sit in the living room and watch television? Oh, *Perry Mason*, oh, *National Barn Dance*, where are you?) The telephone rang. Tom Stafford, in Columbus to do some simulator work at the North American Aviation plant there, was calling to pay his respects to my parents. My answering the phone was pure coincidence. Stafford had little skill and even less concern for small talk. After the customary amenities—how are you, how's the family, and all that—he asked, "Did you get your chit in for the program yet?"

"No," I replied. "Didn't know I could. The article in the paper said only civilians could apply."

"No, hell no, that's not right!" he exclaimed. "Sounds like the news weenies got the garbled word. The selections are open to anybody that meets the qualifications. But you better hurry if you want in on it. The deadline for applications is next week."

"Next week! I'm going to be on leave till next week. Besides, I won't have any chance anyway. I turned down a chance to go back to Edwards for that space pilot course. I figure that screws the works as far as the air force is concerned," I said with resignation.

"It won't hurt you that much, Donn," Tom asserted. "There have only been about fifteen guys go through that space thing and most of them are too old, too tall, or not interested. And if you get past the air force you'd have a damn good chance with NASA."

"Well, I suppose as good as anybody,"

"Hell, yes. You're the only guy I know of who's been through the test pilot school and has an MS in astronautics."

"You're right. I hadn't thought of it that way. Guess I'll have to go back off leave early and get my chit in."

"So suffer a little," Tom chortled.

"Yeah, man. I'll see ya."

"So long."

Mom got on the phone and invited Tom to dinner. He was busy flying the simulator, he said, but would call later if he could arrange his schedule to come to dinner. It was the old keep-'em-on-the-string-but-don't-commit-yourself trick that I learned later is practiced with great skill by astronauts. The idea was to hold off for a better deal: a swinging time on the town at someone else's expense, a good or at least a sure lay, a chance to hobnob with big shots and celebrities. Tom declined her invitation on the premise that his simulator schedule was too erratic to permit planning ahead for any social activities.

The next morning I called my office at Kirtland Air Base. Yes, a message had come in concerning astronaut applications to NASA, John Sexton said, but they had surmised I wasn't interested since I had turned down the other deal at Edwards. I told him I *was* interested and would he please tell our administrative people to start pulling together the information I would need for the application. People there really *moved* for me. If it had not been for the guys in administration and personnel, I would never have made it. And if Tom had not called me, I would never have bothered.

To meet the deadline we returned to New Mexico a few days early. I didn't mind. It was a good excuse to get the hell out of Ohio. I had fulfilled the customary filial obligations: attended Masonic lodge with my father, met all the neighbors, watched *Lawrence Welk* and refrained from calling it the *Lawrence Belch Show* because my mother would get upset. Later, after becoming an astronaut, I would submit myself to the embarrassment of having my identity announced to disinterested strangers in restaurants, on ferry boats, and other public places by my mother. I learned to suffer tolerantly through the attendant fuss and commotion. The potted palm syndrome knows no limits. Proud, beaming parents persist in public display of prized offspring, even when the progeny have reached their middle years of maturity.

Our circumstances were more relaxed in Harriet's home town of Gnadenhutten, a small and picturesque village nestled among the hills of eastern Ohio. But days of peace and quiet soon become endless hours of boredom, and one chafes at incessant inactivity. Actually, in her parents' home there was continual calamity and a succession of minor uproars, but there were ample escapes from the turmoil and I seldom got drawn into it.

I hurried back to Albuquerque and hustled to get my application sent in before the deadline. Over two hundred air force pilots applied, and about three weeks later the air force published a list of twenty-six names that they were forwarding to NASA. Shortly afterward NASA announced the results of their preliminary screening: there were thirty-four candidates, including fourteen of the air force twenty-six. I noted with satisfaction that Bassett, Freeman, myself, and several of our former Edwards colleagues were included. The NASA announcement also instructed the selectees to report to the Air Force Aeromedical Center at Brooks Air Force Base in San Antonio for weeklong physical examinations.

3. Astronaut Selection

The week at Brooks Air Force Base was the most exhaustive—and exhausting—physical I have ever had or heard of. It offered all the delights and comforts of a medieval inquisition. Within the chambers of horrors there, we discovered a variety of diabolical devices and procedures. No doubt all were necessary for a rigorous assessment of one's physical condition, but I couldn't help feeling that some were too severe and overdone. Of course in our mindless zeal to become astronauts, none of us candidates were about to complain. The tolerance and endurance of strong-willed, disciplined, and highly motivated men is quite beyond measure or rationality. We would have eaten the proverbial feces with a rusty spoon had an act of such degradation been required.

We were told that the examinations were not comparative, that the main purpose was to ensure a slate of candidates who were as free as possible from physical defects and incipient or potential infirmities. Nevertheless we competed vigorously whenever possible. The infamous treadmill, a device for testing the heart and lungs under extreme duress, was a prime example. The idea was to stay on as long as possible while the treadmill elevated to progressively higher inclinations—about one degree a minute. The treadmill moved at about three miles an hour, a nice brisk walk, but the cumulative effort of fifteen or twenty minutes' walking up an ever steeper hill was sufficient to exhaust all but the most energetic and superbly conditioned specimens.

The procedure began with attendants pasting sensors and taping wires to the subject's body. The wires were attached to long leads that carried the sensor signals to a number of recording mechanisms. The test subject would gather the bundle of wires, draped loosely through his hands to prevent pulling loose the sensors but held high enough to avoid entangling his feet and legs, and step onto the treadmill. Then the fun began. The first sign of physical exertion appeared at six or eight minutes: heavy breathing and beads of sweat standing on the forehead. By fifteen minutes the chest was heaving, sweat ran down the body in rivulets, and the face flushed beet-red. The test was supposed to continue until the blood pressure reached 240, the pulse registered 200 beats a minute, or to the point of exhaustion, whichever occurred first.

One minute before the end—one was expected to predict or anticipate when he had precisely one minute's worth of stamina remaining—an attendant would shove a rubber mouthpiece into the mouth and clamp the nose shut. During that last minute all the air one exhaled went into a large gray rubber bag. At the climactic conclusion of this frightful experience, the machinery stopped as the subject collapsed gratefully into the waiting arms of two medical corpsmen while another whisked the breath balloon, now swollen to about four feet across, to the gas analysis laboratory. If the candidate elected to get off the treadmill prematurely, either he was out of condition or he wasn't trying very hard. Most of us found the whole procedure trying—very trying indeed. It was a great point of pride and competition to see who could stay on the treadmill the longest. From the standpoint of its medical value there was no need to carry the treadmill test to such extremes. But working to exhaustion was imperative to satisfy our competitive compulsions.

There were other treats in store. The barium milk shake, a tumbler of thick tasteless milky glop, chalkier and more disgusting than milk of magnesia, had to be gulped down to render the gut more amenable to x-ray examination. It would not do for one's innards to harbor any secrets from the examining physicians. In the glucose tolerance test one had to swallow on an absolutely empty stomach—twelve-hour fasting was required—about ten ounces of pure liquid sugar: a syrupy, sickening-sweet transparent mess. The impulse to retch was overpowering. Several fellows threw up immediately and had to drink another glass of the vile sick-sweetness. If they tossed the second batch, they had to wait and try again another day. If one could retain the sugar, he first felt a terrible disturbance in the belly, as if someone had punched him in the solar plexus. Next came waves of nausea followed by lightheadedness and a vague dizzy sensation. Usually all color drained from his face and cold sweat beaded his livid brow. Assuming he could tolerate all that discomfort, the candidate was privileged to have his arm punctured at thirty-minute intervals for blood samples.

The tilt table had all the charm of a medieval torture rack. The test subject lay face-up on a table, his body secured by straps at the crotch and armpits. His body was liberally laced with wires and sensors. The table tilted to the vertical and the candidate was allowed to hang, suspended with his full weight on the crotch straps, for forty-five minutes—or until he passed out from having his blood circulation cut off.

For the electroencephalograph, one had to submit to having his scalp pierced with twenty or thirty pins, each taped in place and properly wired to carry signals to the brain wave machine. The idea was to sit back and relax in an easy chair for half an hour or so while the attending medic took measurements. Despite the dull aching in my scalp, I overdid the relaxation and fell asleep. This merciful respite ended with the attendant hollering at me to wake up. He revised his instructions: try to relax, but don't get *too* relaxed.

We also submitted ourselves to the indignities of the proctoscope, a foot-long steel tube inserted into the rectum to permit visual inspection of the lower bowel. To prepare for this examination, we first took an enema or perhaps several. Then, stripped nude, we mounted a contraption that held the body in a sort of inverted fetal position: knees flexed, legs spread, head down, buttocks up. I've never felt more ridiculous. The doctor then inserted the instrument (ooh, it's cold!) called the steel eel, silver bugle, and other terms of endearment. The internist who examined me was an enthusiastic fellow given to lively exclamations of oohs and aahs as he proceeded.

"Beautiful!" he cried. "Fantastic! Your bowel is superb. Clean as a whistle!"

When we had finished I was most relieved to get my superb clean ass the hell out of there.

During our week at Brooks we were probed, punctured, thumped, felt, listened to, and looked at by two dozen physicians and perhaps fifty medical technicians. We had ice water poured in our ears and got sick and dizzy from a rotating, tilting chair. Psychological testing took up about one full day. We responded to IQ tests, filled out psychological questionnaires, imagined the appropriate bears and butterflies on the Rorschach ink blots, gave impressions and made up stories about a series of peculiar dreary pictures, and consulted with a psychiatrist. They took our brains apart as well as our bodies. Saturday morning we were released to return to our homes and jobs while we awaited word of the outcome of what must be the most thorough and extensive examination of eminently healthy people ever conducted.

Six of the thirty-four candidates were dropped on account of their physical exams at Brooks. The remaining twenty-eight in mid-August of 1963 received confidential instructions to come to Houston for interviews and technical exams. We all made our way as unobtrusively as possible to Houston where our arrival was treated with marked circumspection. Manned Spacecraft Center officials met us at the gate in the airport and furtively escorted us to waiting limousines that sped us downtown to the Rice Hotel, an elderly edifice striving desperately to preserve its elegance of years past. There we were handed over to other men who took us up a rear elevator directly to our rooms, where we discovered we had been registered under assumed names. I was Clyde Pepper from Corpus Christi. The whole affair seemed like a comic episode from a Gilbert and Sullivan opera. Or like a scene from one of those dreadful old spy serials I used to see at the movies on Saturday afternoon when I was a kid.

The reason for this skulking about, we were told, was to keep the pesky news reporters from interfering with the interviews and generally mucking up the selection proceedings. Later I came to realize that the space agency held a curiously condescending and occasionally negative attitude toward newsmen. There seemed to be an unspoken and tacitly accepted policy that the public relations function should serve principally to project what the NASA chieftains believed was the proper image of esoteric infallibility. Informing the public, translating the bewildering complexities of space technology into the vernacular, was incidental. Operating under the aegis of Messrs. Kennedy and Johnson with the able and wholehearted support of a group of powerful legislators, the agency saw little need to deign to explain itself. "We would like to tell you what we are doing, but we're too busy and you wouldn't understand anyway." The public, boggling at the profluence of spectacular feats in space, was too dazzled to want to comprehend the technicalities, too awed to criticize the rationale or to question the space program's basic purpose.

Among the NASAites most contemptuous of reporters were a large number of astronauts, principally but not exclusively the Mercury ones—the so-called "original seven," a term that to this day infuriates the other non-Mercury astronauts. Perhaps they suffered from their image of superiority or cherished their mystique too much. Whatever their hang-ups, the astronauts were loath to chance the revelation of their human imperfections through exposure to public news media. Despite their formidable self-discipline and emotional control, those men became remarkably insecure at any real or imagined threat to their image.

The astronauts' wives would comprise an interesting group subject for psychological study. It was interesting to see how they coped, or failed to cope, with the life-roles thrust upon them when their husbands became astronauts. Most of these pitiable women were ill equipped to handle the pressures of public attention and interest focused upon them. Some became haughty and patronizing out of heightened conceit over their suddenly elevated status. They were given to blatant displays of arrogance, apparently in the belief that their exalted station warranted the whole world's bending over to buss their pampered backsides.

Other astrowives reacted rather differently. These *misérables* felt so overwhelmed by it all that they tended to run and hide from reporters, photographers, or even large parties where strangers might take some notice of them. Their penchant for anonymity reached neurotic proportions. The ones who were naturally shy and reticent became withdrawn and reclusive.

The majority of these women felt like fish out of water. In an attempt to reimmerse themselves in the pond of mediocrity and banal middle-classness from which they had swum, a number of wretches went to great lengths to demonstrate that they were, really, still jes' plain folks like everybody else. Their various adaptive defense mechanisms of arrogance, compulsive shyness, and strained egalitarianism served to mask these women's deep-seated insecurities and constituted massive self- and mutual delusion. Their private anxieties and personal hang-ups became aggregate neuroses of monumental proportions.

I had come to Houston with my brain crammed full of technical tidbits and data on aeronautics and spaceflight gleaned from textbooks and oracles of the trade like *Aviation Week*: Newton's laws of motion, Kepler's law of gravitation, theories and principles of airplane flight control and performance, gyroscopes, rocket engines, technical details of Gemini spacecraft, gyroscopic precession-impulse momentum theory, the gamut of astronautical topics—I was ready.

Our first formal gathering was relaxed and sociable, with Deke Slayton presiding in a low-key, off-the-cuff, shucks-fellers manner. Wally Schirra bounced in briefly to make a few jovial remarks that confused more than amused us. I was terribly impressed, as I'm sure were the other candidates. After this brief chummy welcome we began our written exams. I was disappointed at the questions—not at all what I expected, hardly concerned with all the vast amounts of technical material I had labored so arduously to assimilate. The test was rather general and subjective, and seemed more geared to trying our talents for self-expression and examining our attitudes than to measuring the breadth of our technical knowledge. Drat! All those colorful facts and figures, all those hours of cramming, gone to waste!

Our next function was to meet the selection board for personal interviews. At the appointed time I arrived promptly, dressed in a black suit with narrow lapels, a skinny dark tie, and a white shirt. You couldn't get any more decorous, conservative, or nondescript than that, I figured. And nondescript attire was *de rigueur* for those who toiled in the space biz in the early sixties. And still is, for many. The style of dress of these men matched their mediocre style of living. Banal existence gave nice, formless counterpoint to the narrow brilliance of their mentalities.

I was ushered from the outer reception room to the inner sanctum. There, all in a row, sat five moguls of spaceflight. Al Shepard, who smirked sardonically and persistently pierced my skull with darts from his steely blue eyes. Jolly Wally Schirra, crackling with puns and good humor (puns and humor are not necessarily synonymous). Quiet, serious Mr. Slayton. John Glenn, the original Mr. Clean, genuinely a nice fellow despite disparagements uttered about him by some of his astronaut cohorts. And quizzical, inarticulate Warren North, chief of technical and training support for the astronauts. How did he get in here? I wondered.

We shook hands and exchanged pleasantries. I sat down in a chair facing the tribunal. My nerves tingled, my heart raced, my mouth went dry. I was scared stiff, but tried to conceal terror with outward composure. My God, what mere mortal would presume to place himself in the presence of these Olympian giants?

Shepard opened the questioning by asking me what I thought of pilots flying booster rockets right from liftoff all the way to orbit, as opposed to automatic control of the launch trajectory. I mouthed some platitudes about pilot-in-the-loop and man's ability to control, but hedged with rambling discourse on the probable difficulties of implementing such a system, and on booster control reliability. (What the hell am I supposed to say? Should I be for it or against it?) It was obvious to Shepard and the others that I didn't know what I was talking about. He smirked and squinted an expression of devastating disdain that cut me off in mid-sentence. (Aw shit, Al, why don't you ask me about something I know? Something easy, like details of the Gemini spacecraft?)

After a brief awkward silence, Slayton asked me about my flying experience. I gave a brief résumé and went on at some length about my work in Albuquerque. Warren North wanted to know how I did at Edwards. Wally mentioned he had served at China Lake, fifty miles north of Edwards, and asked if I had flown up there. The conversation was getting quite sociable and I began to relax. John Glenn observed that we were both Ohioans, and we engaged in a little "Who do you know?" and "Do you remember . . . ?"

Then Shepard started in again. "You went to the Naval Academy. What class?"

"Nineteen fifty-two," I answered.

"What prompted you to go into the air force?" he continued.

"Well, at the time there wasn't an Air Force Academy yet, and they used to take a fourth of each class—"

"I'm aware of all that!" he interrupted testily. I got the impression I had insulted him. "Why did you choose the air force instead of the navy?"

"Well, frankly, I didn't get along too well there, and all I knew of the navy was what I saw at the Naval Academy. I decided I'd rather be in the air force."

It was obvious I had committed a grievous blunder. "And just what the hell is wrong with the navy?" he rasped, glowering.

I became defensive. Shepard had me nailed and I was squirming and he knew it. "Nothing is wrong with the navy. The naval service is a fine outfit and knowing what I know now, if I had to do it over, I might go the other way."

"Then you think you made a bad decision?"

"No, not really. I've had a nice career in the air force—gotten to do just about everything I've wanted to. It's just that after eleven years the reasons for that decision don't seem so important as they were then."

"And just exactly what were those reasons?" Al asked impatiently.

"Well. I, ah, wanted to fly and I didn't care for sea duty. And like I said I had kind of a tough time at Annapolis, and—"

"What do you mean, a tough time?" he interjected with exasperation. "Didn't you stand pretty high in your class?"

"Yes, I did. The top 10 or 15 percent, I think. Never had any trouble, really, with grades. At least academic grades. I made stars most of the time. And there were a lot of nice extracurricular things—athletics, clubs, and so forth. But I didn't do so hot in conduct and aptitude. Seemed to be at odds with the system all the time. There were so many petty and senseless rules whose sole purpose seemed to be to make life difficult for the midshipmen." By this time Shepard was doing a slow burn. His face flushed and his eyes narrowed into slits. "But Annapolis is a great school," I hastened to add, albeit unconvincingly. "I wouldn't trade my education, and the training there, for anything. It's great preparation for a career in any of the services—or for civilian life, for that matter."

Having been thoroughly unnerved by Shepard's contemptuous needling, I was about to lapse further into frenetic garrulousness when Wally came to my rescue. "What did you fly at Edwards?" he asked, switching subjects abruptly and taking me off the hook with Shepard.

"Let's see . . . T-33s, T-38, T-28, and B-57s. Oh, and one flight in a T-39. That's a nice airplane. Flies like an F-86."

We talked on briefly about different airplanes and how they flew. I answered a few incidental questions from Glenn and Slayton. The conversations dwindled and Slayton announced, "I guess that's about it. We better tie this off if we're going to keep on schedule. So, if nobody's got any more questions . . ." He paused, looked around. No one spoke. I tensed in fear of more skewers from Shepard, but Al said nothing. "Okay, Donn, thanks a lot," Deke said. "We'll get in touch with you later."

I, Donn Eisele, alias Clyde Pepper of Corpus Christi, wandered back to my secret chamber at the Rice Hotel feeling defeated, a little dazed, and thoroughly disgusted with myself. You dumb bastard, I thought, how could you let Shepard get to you like that? You blew it! Your one big chance, and you blew it, bigger than hell! He and the rest of those guys must think you're the world's biggest idiot. I was to find out later that Shepard had a similarly disturbing effect on a lot of others.

Tom and Faye Stafford had invited me to dine and spend the evening at their home. Late that afternoon Tom picked me up in front of the Rice in his new Corvair. He explained that the car was the next thing to a gift from General Motors. Certain GM officials had wanted to give cars to astronauts, but the space pilots were not permitted to accept them. An alternate was worked out whereby the astronauts were allowed to purchase new Chevrolets at dealers' cost less 10 percent, the same privilege accorded new car salesmen. The automobiles could be financed with one-year balloon notes: token payments monthly with the preponderant amount due at the end. And at the end of the year the cars could be sold at virtually no loss—sometimes at a profit—a new car purchased, and the cycle repeated.

An ironic anecdote with respect to cars was the episode in St. Louis when Stafford and some other astronauts were treated to the use of courtesy cars by a local Oldsmobile dealer. A reporter there got wind of it and published the story. When the matter came to Administrator Webb's attention, he became incensed and summarily demanded that the errant spacemen thereafter use only authorized rental cars at government expense. After all, gratuities were prohibited!

I returned to Albuquerque with mixed feelings of hope and futility. I'd been through all the screening processes, the tests, and the interviews, and when it was over the people at NASA said that they'd let me know. Well, naturally I was very eager to be accepted, but when about three months went by without hearing from them it seemed that perhaps they just didn't want me.

Prospects dimmed as the weeks went by with no word from NASA. I had all but given up when one afternoon Deke Slayton phoned and said something casual like, "Donn, we have selected you to be an astronaut. Would you like to come down to Houston and join the group?"

I was stunned. This was it! Just like that. One simple phone call, and I was an astronaut. My God, I'm an astronaut! In an instant, it seemed, I had been propelled from nondescript anonymity to professional prominence. "Oh, sure, Deke, I'd like very much to come. Thank you. When do you want me?" I replied with forced nonchalance. My heart raced and I could scarcely contain the excitement, but it seemed important to appear cool.

"Be here next Wednesday. We're going to announce it publicly on Thursday and present you gents to the press. Your plane ticket is in the mail. We'll meet you at the airport. And listen, keep this under your hat. We don't want it to leak out 'til we're ready."

4. Going Back to Houston

Bill Anders and I rode together on the plane from Albuquerque. One of NASA's administrative gumshoes met us at the Houston airport and whisked us away to the Rice Hotel. The next day, NASA dignitaries greeted the fourteen new astronauts. There were handshakes, congratulations, and publicity photos taken all around. In the afternoon we presented ourselves to the public at a press conference at an auditorium somewhere in Houston. Never before had I seen so many cameras in one place. Fifty, perhaps a hundred photographers and reporters sat down front. Several TV cameras stared at us from an elevated platform halfway back. A gaggle of onlookers filtered into the rows of seats toward the back and sides.

Intense white light from flood lamps pressed down upon the open stage. We could feel the heat as we filed on stage and took our assigned seats at a long table with microphones on it. Flashguns popped in flurries down front. Paul Haney, public relations head for the space center, introduced us one by one and gave brief biographies. All but two were military pilots, and most of us were engineering test pilots. Rusty Schweickart and Walt Cunningham were billed as scientists, but both were pilots in military reserve outfits.

Questions from the reporters were the usual ones: Why do you want to be an astronaut? What do you think the future will be for space? Do you want to go to the moon? Do you think you will? We all answered each question, one at a time, in alphabetical order. It took quite a while. By the time it got to C.C. Williams, there wasn't much left to say, but he managed a couple of good quips. Rusty said he had always wanted to go to the moon, which sounded like a lot of crap to me. Who would even have thought of it until a few years ago? He didn't exactly endear himself to other astronauts by saying he figured he had the best chance because he was a scientist and the youngest astronaut. Buzz Aldrin hinted he might go first. He seemed to feel he was the smartest by virtue of having done his PhD thesis in rendezvous. That attitude didn't sell too well with the more senior astronauts.

Back at home, Harriet and I had sent our couch out to be cleaned. We knew the press would be descending on our home when I returned, and a neighbor said I had to have a couch for that moment, so she loaned us hers. We were carrying a couch across the backyard when the press showed up.

We all returned to Houston the first of February to begin training. In the meantime Harriet and I had bought a lot in El Lago, about three miles from the space center. We had chosen a house plan and gotten construction started. Our lot was next door to John Young, across the street from the Bormans, and down a few doors from the Staffords. Ed White and Neil Armstrong lived next to each other about a block away. The other inhabitants were nearly all NASA people. They were good neighbors and shared our triumphs, trials, and frustrations. In emergencies they were always at hand to help out. But it did get pretty dull, with everybody being at NASA and not having much else to talk about.

My house was nothing extraordinary, just a typical suburban dwelling with the customary provisions, all done up in traditional architecture with brick and wood façade. But after all those years living in bare housing and nondescript rentals, I felt like a king in his palace. Since I was gone a lot it took several years for the novelty to wear off and the deadly boredom of suburbia's banal tedium to set in.

Our training consisted of classroom work and simulator flying in Houston and frequent field trips. They kept us holed up in classrooms most of the time, at first. Astronomy, the physics of spaceflight, aerodynamics, communications, rocket propulsion, computer theory, space biology—it seemed like we studied everything. Then after a while we started traveling. We made the rounds to other NASA centers at Huntsville, Alabama, where Wernher von Braun and his cronies from v2 days still held forth, designing and building the best rockets in the world and dreaming the most incredible, gargantuan schemes for the future; and to the launch center at Cape Kennedy, where we first met a rotating entourage of sociable females.

We took jungle survival training in Panama, and desert survival in Nevada. Panama was fun—about like camping out with a Scout troop—except they didn't give us any food. We had to find our own, in the jungle.

Then there were the geology field trips. From time to time, eight or ten astronauts, two or three geologists, and assorted onlookers would trek off to the wilderness someplace to study rocks. Our first trip was to the Grand Canyon. We walked all the way to the bottom and back out again—about twenty miles straight up and down—to study the rock layers exposed in the canyon walls. Later, we went to other places like Meteor Crater in Arizona, to see how a crater was formed when a huge rock from outer space crashed into the earth, millions of years ago; Hawaii, to study fresh lava beds, still warm and steaming from recent volcanic eruptions; and Iceland, where parts of the country look just like those pictures of the moon you've seen. We went to a lot of different places to study rocks and we learned a great deal about geology in a short time—although I must confess, sometimes all the rocks began to look alike to me. One thing was for sure: to be an astronaut, you had to handle a lot of rocks.

Besides our classes and field trips, we all had technical assignments. Mine was to learn all about the flight control system on Apollo and to work with the engineers who designed them. People don't realize it, but most astronauts spend more time doing technical work than they do training for spaceflights. Among other things, I had to go to a lot of meetings and design reviews on controls, instruments, lights, hatches, crew couches, windows, storage compartments—in fact, just about everything in the cabin.

I flew a lot of spacecraft simulators, too—not so much for training but to help engineers decide what kind of flight control system would be best for different maneuvers or different parts of an Apollo mission. Some simulators were set up to test procedures and controls for landing on the moon. I'll bet I landed on the moon five hundred times—in simulators.

At the Mission Control Center in Houston during a spaceflight, the VIP viewing room was packed solid with the privileged elite of space and government: congressmen, air force generals, corporation heads, astronauts, the NASA administrator, and numerous lesser luminaries of the agency's hierarchy. Security guards in dark blue stood watch outside in the hall to be sure no one entered without the proper green plastic-coated badge. The room, arranged like a theater with several long rows of red fold-down movie seats, allowed the occupants to watch the action in the Mission Operations Control Room (MOCR, pronounced "moker") through a large room-wide clear glass pane. The viewing room seated about 150 persons, and at least that many more crowded into the aisles and on the steps leading up from the doors. The front row of seats was reserved by name for certain congressmen and generals, and a small assortment of senior NASA officials.

Inside the MOCR the flight control teams arranged themselves at tiered rows of consoles, their backs to the spectators on the other side of the glass. The top tier, nearest the window, accommodated the mission director from NASA headquarters, a sort of chairman of the board for the operation; the chief public affairs officer, controlling the flow of transmissions and commentary to the press and TV networks (news reporters were not permitted beyond the first-floor lobby of the Control Center during spaceflights); the senior military officer, usually an air force general, responsible for the military services' support of the flight; and three or four staff assistants.

Loudspeakers mounted flush in the ceiling carried the sounds of the flight director's communications net which included, among other things, voice transmissions to and from the spacecraft when it was in contact.

At the center of the second tier sat the flight director, the chief executive officer of the flight control team and the man most singularly responsible for the mission's safe conduct and successful conclusion. Manning consoles on his left were a communications engineer, the procedures officer, and the flight director's assistant. On the right were one or two mission planners and the network controller, the man who managed a vast and confusing array of communications links among the MOCR denizens and between Mission Control and the far-flung ships and tracking stations of the spaceflight network that relayed voice and data to the spaceship and astronauts in orbit.

The fourth and lowest row of consoles, known affectionately as "the trench," was situated on the ground-floor level of the MOCR. At far left sat the booster engineer, the man who kept track of our Saturn rocket's performance during launch and first ten hours or so of the flight, until the upper stage ran out of electrical power. Next in line, the retro officer kept continuous watch over our orbit path to determine, for every orbit, the best time and place for reentry if we should have to come down early. The results of his calculations were passed up to us in blocks of numbers for five or six revolutions at a time—"block data," we called it. Fortunately we never had to use his services, but it was comforting to know that we were never more than ninety minutes from return to Earth.

Our retro officer was a burly, good-natured Virginian named John

Llewellyn, a man of strong personality and forceful manner who had earned the appellative "super retro" for the accuracy of his calculations and his resounding, boom-voiced countdowns to retro burn. His role would grow more important as the time for *Apollo 7* entry drew near.

Another imposing denizen of the trench was Phil Shaffer, our flight dynamics officer, or FIDO for short. He was a trajectory specialist and flight mechanics expert whose job it was to supervise the flow of trajectory data between the spacecraft's onboard guidance system, the ground-based tracking radars, and the huge banks of computers in the Mission Control Center. Phil was an enormous, bulky man of casual comportment and quiet humor. We called him "The World's Biggest Flight Controller." He also happened to be the best. He could compute our thrusting maneuvers within a fraction of a foot per second and could predict our position at any instant within a few hundred feet of altitude and less than a mile along our flight path. I attribute the success of our rendezvous to his skill and finesse at positioning us for the initial maneuvers.

The flight surgeons resided at their monitoring station on the left of the third level from the top: tall, skeletal Duane Catterson, his large round eyes rolling as he scanned the control room, his bloodless complexion made all the more pallid by the fluorescent lighting, his Adam's apple bobbing visibly in his scrawny neck as he talked; plump, cherubic John Ziegelschmid, smiling fatuously and exuding childlike enthusiasm; and charismatic Charles Berry, chief medical officer at the Manned Spacecraft Center, looking smooth, unruffled, and impeccably groomed as usual. Berry's bland, ingratiating manner and his penchant for publicity and acclaim had propelled his meteoric rise from obscurity as an air force flight surgeon to unassailable preeminence as senior spokesman for space medicine. Berry was not above exploiting his subordinates for his own aggrandizement. And his skill at intramural politics projected a favorable image that laid a velvety façade over the rubble of discontent and confusion that sprung from his inept and high-handed leadership.

Berry allowed himself to be billed as the "astronauts' physician," despite the fact he seldom saw them and never personally administered treatment or examinations. But it was not in his character to correct the misapprehension by volunteering the names of the unsung doctors who really did the work. The turnover in flight surgeons was fierce. Military men assigned there stayed only the minimum time required. The civilians, who enjoyed more latitude, left even sooner. Of all the dozens of doctors who came to the Manned Spacecraft Center over the years, a half dozen or so remained to serve as Berry's minions and to form the nucleus of his deadening and stultifying bureaucracy. These were passive, unimaginative men whose servile natures and utter lack of messianic hang-ups that afflict many physicians fit well with their circumstances; or men whose fascination with spaceflight overrode any bruising of egos they otherwise might have felt.

Most astronauts maintained an arm's-length, coolly cordial relationship with Berry. His duplicitous and politically motivated behavior engendered mistrust, and his years away from clinical medicine rendered his medical competence suspect. Most astronauts would have flatly refused treatment by him. They also resented his intrusion into whatever personal confidences they had formed with working flight surgeons. Berry insisted on knowing every detail of even the most inconsequential illness or injury, and any physician who presumed to confound Berry's omniscience fared poorly in the medical hierarchy.

This intrusion in turn inhibited the formation of trust and confidence between flight crews and their surgeons because Berry was in the habit of making public announcements concerning the health and medical problems of astronauts—details of a personal nature that ought to have been kept confidential. Berry's propensity to mouth all to the press only served to intensify the traditional paranoia—fear of grounding, really—that all aviators are prone to. And public exposure of medical problems tended to tarnish the image of invincibility, at least in the insecure minds of some of the astronauts. As a result, many of them sought whatever medical care they required from sources outside NASA and with no knowledge or concurrence of Berry or his underlings.

My own encounter with Chuck Berry's publicity syndrome occurred at the time I had surgery on my left shoulder for recurrent dislocations. About six months after I joined the astronaut corps, I dislocated my shoulder when I fell down during a zero-g airplane flight. (Dick Gordon and I were clowning around.) A year later I threw my shoulder out again while playing handball. After hemming and hawing for several months, Berry finally decreed I had to have surgery to be cleared for spaceflight. I got the word, not from his nibs himself, but at a conclave of several of his subalterns. The medics said, "That's all, bud. If you want to fly in space, go to the hospital and get your arm fixed so it won't come out again."

Two weeks before I went in, Gus Grissom told me I was going to be on the first Apollo with him and Ed White. I walked on air for a few days until Slayton brought me down with the news that I couldn't be on the first Apollo because of my forthcoming arm operation. It seemed our good doctors couldn't guarantee a full recovery or a recuperative period of less than six months—it actually took less than two. Deke did, however, assign me to the second Apollo flight with Walt Cunningham and Wally Schirra.

I wanted as little fuss over the matter as possible since my future as an astronaut hinged on the success of the operation. The mere fact I had to have it seemed bad enough. On the appointed day I quietly entered a Houston hospital, having told a few of my close friends and associates that I would be out of touch for a few days. The evening television news carried the story of my impending surgery and quoted Dr. Berry as the source. Then, two days—less than forty-eight hours—after the operation, Berry called me to ask if it would be all right for some photographers and reporters from the news pool (representing all the major news services) to get pictures of me lying in the hospital. And of course Berry would accompany them, to help answer questions. I told him I'd rather not do it right then, but that he could check it out with Slayton. I felt pretty rotten—still in considerable pain and under sedation from time to time—and thought Berry had a hell of a nerve asking me to submit to crap like that so soon after surgery. I figured that going through Slayton would take another two or three days and with a little luck I'd be out of the hospital by then. My timing was perfect. I checked out at noon on the day the photographers were supposed to come at one o'clock.

Several months later the second Apollo flight got canceled—it was a repeat of the first flight, mostly—and the three of us were out of it.

It was interesting to see how it all evolved. There had been some sentiment all along to scrub our flight since it was so much like Gus's, but we all resisted until we ran into a snag on simulators and a few other things. That's when Wally started to howl and say that we couldn't meet the launch date due to inadequate training. Wally's written ultimatum to Deke—"We won't fly unless . . ."—served to tip the scales, and we lost the flight.

Meanwhile, Wally maneuvered behind the scenes to cop the next flight in line. It was to be the first of the Lunar Module flights. Wally would rather have had that one in the first place. It piqued his ego to have to play second fiddle to Gus. He had pulled a similar power play before, in Gemini, to get the first rendezvous flight. But this time it backfired. McDivitt's crew, who had been backup for Gus, Ed, and Roger, moved over to the prime crew slot for the first LM mission. We took McDivitt's place as backup for Gus. Now we were *really* second fiddle. And worst of all we had no promise or prospect for a subsequent prime crew assignment.

Then came the fire, and all its gory aftermath. Only a month before its scheduled flight date, a flash fire on the launch pad destroyed the space-craft and took the lives of the three astronauts who were to fly it. Everyone involved with the flight went into shock at first, but then we got to work try-ing to find out what caused the fire and how to make the next spaceship safe.

5. After the Fire

Walt and I got involved in the post-fire investigation. Wally copped out—in retrospect, a wise move. The first thing we had to do was listen to voice tapes and try to identify who said what in the spacecraft when the fire broke out. Did you ever listen to your friends scream in panic, then agony, as they fry to death? Listen to it over and over and over again? I don't know why we did it—I guess it seemed terribly important at the time to find out who said what.

Then I spent some time in the spacecraft cabin—what was left of it—trying to help the fire experts identify bits and pieces of charred and melted material. The acrid smell of burned plastic, paint, and nylon was overpowering. There were little piles of debris all over the floor and the crew couches. The side walls and the instrument panels were charred, discolored, and warped from the heat. The mess in the cabin and the screaming on the voice tapes gave me nightmares at first. But after a while the dreams went away, along with the knot in my stomach.

At first we didn't know what would happen to the three of us, personally, or to the program. But plans soon jelled, and everything fell into place. The Apollo program would continue, but the first flight would be delayed at least a year in order to make changes in the spacecraft that were necessary to make it safe from fire and better equipped for moon flights. And Wally, Walt, and I were asked to make the first flight.

One day Slayton came up to us in the hall at Kennedy Space Center and told us we were to fly the first Apollo if we wanted it. We said, "Hell, yes, we want it!" But we were determined to have a good spacecraft this time around, not another bucket of bolts like Gus, Ed, and Roger's. Our confidence was shot but we knew it would come back if NASA and North American Aviation could show us a good spacecraft.

The real tragedy of the 204 fire was that it was so preventable, so unnecessary—almost criminal, in fact. The incredibly incompetent management, which, in my opinion, led to the fire, arose out of George Mueller's naive stupidity and Joe Shea's colossal ego. Mueller was Manned Spaceflight chief at NASA headquarters, and Shea was Apollo manager at NASA in Houston. Mueller would dictate some impossible schedules for spacecraft delivery, checkout, and launch. Shea was vain enough to think he could meet them. And the contractors were dishonest or equally stupid, or both, for not telling NASA they couldn't hack it.

Two years before the fire, a number of astronauts and engineers petitioned Shea to approve a simple, one-piece, outward-opening hatch design in place of the awkward two-piece hatch panel we had then. Not only was it cumbersome to handle, it sealed from the inside of the cabin, which meant that any slight overpressure in the cabin—like in a fire—would plaster it against its seals so hard you couldn't pull it loose with elephants. I remember looking at Ed White's finger scrapings in the melted goo on the inner hatch surface. He must have pawed frantically, trying to get the hatch open, just seconds before he expired from searing hot gases that suffocated him and burned out his lungs.

Shea turned us down. "Too much money and not enough time," he said. "It's a 'crew comfort' item. You guys are just too lazy to wrestle with the hatch we've got. What the hell, it works, doesn't it?" It's ironic that the first major change made to the spacecraft after the *Apollo 1* fire was the simple, one-piece hatch we had asked for two years earlier. And you should have seen the North American weenies. They crowed about the "new" hatch until one would think they had invented the wheel.

I really believe Joe Shea thought we were sandbagging about the hatch. He seemed to have a peculiarly contemptuous suspicion of astronauts, anyway. How could dumb-ass pilots know anything? Most of them didn't even have PhDs! I think he was also secretly envious. He was ambitious, aggressive, and competitive. He could be devastatingly sarcastic: yet his humor was warm and witty and he could be a most charming fellow on occasion. Joe tried to beat us at everything—handball, running, cracking puns, arm wrestling, even flying our own simulators. He didn't do badly for a beginner. Joe was a good manager except for one fatal fault: he let his ego interfere with his good judgment.

In the ensuing weeks there was some finger-pointing, but surprisingly little considering the circumstances. The North American guys told what a great company they were and what a terrific job they had done on Apollo but allowed as how they might be able to spruce up a bit on management control and test discipline. The NASA guys—the investigating board and others—were pretty honestly critical of themselves and the contractor. Jim Webb, the administrator for NASA, stood up and took the brunt of it before Congress. Wily, weaselly little George Mueller sat tight, didn't say a word, and came through unscathed—at least for the time being. Joe Shea became the scapegoat and got canned.

After that, things got better. The contractor—principally North American—and NASA managements became more open and honest with each other, the spacecraft was redesigned (we got the one-piece hatch and a great many other improvements that were sorely needed), and people started telling George Mueller what they could do and when they could get it done, instead of the other way around as it had been before the fire.

For the next several months we worked with the engineers and mechanics who were building our spacecraft, Number 101, at the plant in California. Our confidence was shot at first on account of the fire, but it gradually returned when we saw what a fine job they were doing. Because of all the spacecraft changes (which had to be done, really, if we were going to fly one of those things to the moon) we had to spend a lot of time at the North American plant in Downey, California, conferring with their designers and engineers and taking part in all the checkout and testing that had to go on before the craft could be sent to Florida. That helped us learn a lot about the spacecraft and gain more confidence in it, the people who built it and checked it out, and those who were helping us prepare for the flight. In fact, we never did turn loose of the testing altogether and concentrate only on training.

It all paid off. But it really got to be a drag sometimes. We'd sit around all week waiting for a test to start. Then just as we got ready to leave for Houston for the weekend, they'd run it. In retrospect we weren't very efficient in managing our own time—it's hard to get much training done when you're hanging fire for a test to start. But the simulators weren't up to speed for us to train on them yet, and I guess we learned as much about the spacecraft by working on it as we would have in a classroom. And then we knew it would be a long time to launch date, anyway. The whole crew, prime, backup, and support, used to sit around and make bets on test startup dates and times, delivery date and launch date. Ed Givens won the launch date pool, but didn't live to collect. He was killed in a car accident in 1967.

We were determined to follow the spacecraft every step of the way, from the day we were assigned to it until the day we flew it. Our confidence was shattered at first by the fire and we knew the only way to get it back was to watch each step in the design-build-test cycle to be sure it got done right. And to raise hell if it wasn't. As it turned out we didn't have to do too much yelling.

One thing that raised our hopes was a guy named John Healey. When North American reshuffled their management they brought in a lot of new people, including Healey, who became spacecraft manager for our ship. By job charter and force of personality, Healey wielded a pretty big stick around there. What North American needed desperately was someone to really be in charge for a change. And if there was ever anybody in charge of anything, it would have to be John Healey. He was magnificent. After an initial period of mutual skepticism, our crew and Healey developed a working rapport and close friendship that endured through the years, long after we left NASA.

We played some pretty neat tricks after-hours in LA. There was always a gathering of engineers, PR guys, and secretaries at the bar at the Tahitian Village Motel, the Dixie Belle restaurant, and the Sandpiper bar in Downey. These convivial assemblies were always good for a few laughs, a few drinks, and dinner on either the proprietors or the North American PR guys, and an occasional lay. With one or two notable exceptions, we didn't fool around much with the North American girls. One that comes to mind was the incident where one of our guys got a North American girl pregnant. The company very suavely sent her off to have an abortion, all expenses paid.

One other time, three or four of us went to Las Vegas overnight from LA along with a couple of PR types and three or four local beauties from Downey. We went in the company airplane. The guy in charge wanted to induct Frank Sinatra into a fighter pilots' organization that he was busy founding. Now, Sinatra never flew a plane in his life, as far as I know, but according to our host, Frank had something called "the fighter pilot spirit," whatever the hell that is. Sinatra wasn't even there, as it turned out, but nobody really cared. I guess we were along because our host needed a few astronaut bodies to lend awe and dignity to the occasion. We were also a great excuse for the PR guys to go out and whoop it up on company funds.

After a while we began to fan out away from Downey, heading south to Newport and Long Beach, then swinging west and north around the coast through Palos Verdes, the west beaches, and up to Santa Monica. We covered a lot of ground, including Hollywood and the Hills of Beverly. There was *gold* in them thar hills.

We had some great times and met some very groovy people—movie stars, entertainers, and big shots in showbiz. We met some real losers, too. Most of these were guys and girls attracted to astronauts like flies. Most seemed to be four-flushers and penny-ante businessmen who fawned on them. There was the golden young swinging Hollywood lawyer who got three years in jail for stealing objects of art from his friends' and clients' homes. I guess he needed the money to support himself and his friends in the style to which he would have liked to become accustomed.

We used to have some great times on comedian Bill Dana's boat. We didn't go anywhere in it—I'm not sure Billy knew how to operate it. But it made a great place for a party or a quiet afternoon. Then there were the broads. There must be at least ten million sexy good-looking women in Southern California. We were accused of trying to get around to all of them. I don't think we did.

The spacecraft finally got rebuilt and tested and shipped to Cape Kennedy via the Aero Spacelines pregnant guppy, a large bulbous airplane capable of carrying Saturn rocket stages. The whole plant went bananas on delivery day. They lived and breathed schedules, and it was a point of pride with Healey and the others that it should go on schedule. I don't know why they were so frantic that day. I guess it was an emotional response en masse to their collective anxieties over shipping on time. I think it was also an outlet for their immense relief, their satisfaction, and their utter glee at having *finally* after all those years completed the first manned Apollo spacecraft.

During those last few months the spacecraft was at Downey, the tempo of our activity picked up. There were the usual day-to-day technical problems that somehow became more critical and demanded more of our attention as delivery date approached. We spent more time in the spacecraft running the integrated systems tests. And our training simulators in Houston and Florida began to support us more predictably. Budgeting our time among the three locations became a problem. We wanted to take advantage of the training opportunities, yet we still wanted to keep close tabs on the progress of our spacecraft. It seems we spent an inordinate amount of time just flying back and forth across the continent. Twelve- and fourteen-hour workdays became routine.

We had plenty of help, of course. There was the backup crew, plus three other astronauts who made up our astronaut support crew. And we had a flight crew support team of about a dozen engineers that took care of an awful lot of details for us. But there are a lot of things you just can't or don't want to delegate. This was to be the first spacecraft of a new and unproven design. And, coming on the heels of the fire, we knew the fate and future of the entire manned space program—not to mention our own skins—was riding on the success or failure of *Apollo 7*.

Looking back, it seems we could have been more efficient. Part of the problem was Wally. He was a great inspirational leader. But he was terribly disorganized personally and really didn't have much talent for management. Yet he would delegate hardly any of his authority—which, as spacecraft crew commander and just because he was Wally Schirra, was considerable. He insisted on making nearly all the decisions.

Most of the time he wouldn't even let Walt or me confer with the program managers unless we cleared it with him first. Wally always said he "didn't want to get bogged down in details." I think this was a cop-out to cover the fact that he was in over his head, and couldn't comprehend or assimilate the complexities of the Apollo spacecraft design. He left the detailed knowledge of operating the spacecraft to Walt and me. That left him free to think big and philosophize and to big-deal it with the higher echelons of management and other persons of prominence. On those rare occasions when he did allow himself to delve into details, he got hung up on dead issues or else he would go off on tangents and never resolve the issues at hand.

It was difficult to get Wally into the simulator, and if he did get in to keep him there. Without realizing it he let everything else take priority. He was forever responding to telephone calls on matters largely irrelevant to the preparations and training for *Apollo 7*. Or he would get into meandering long-winded bull sessions of little consequence. And before every simulator session he would insist on a briefing by the instructors. We often spent more time in the briefings than we did in the simulator itself.

On most flight crews the commander is simply a leader chosen from among peers. Wally saw his role a little differently. He was the captain of a ship and Walt and I were the crew. He had absolute authority. I was the ship's navigator on the bridge and sometime-executive officer. Walt was the crew in the engine compartment.

Another of Wally's preoccupations was his role and position vis-à-vis the flight directors, program managers, and other flight crew commanders. He concerned himself greatly with his image as an authority figure and the pomp and protocol of his position and military rank. He was very jealous of his prerogatives in an environment where they tended largely to get lost in the general tenor of informality and casual camaraderie.

Wally was very much concerned with form and appearances, or "showmanship" as he chose to call it. To him it was more important to look good than to be good. Whenever he possibly could he staged things to cast the most favorable light on Wally Schirra, regardless of whether it was in the best interests of the mission or what effects it had on someone else.

In short, Wally's leadership left much to be desired. When he kept a tight grip on the reins his direction was erratic, ambiguous, and arbitrary, and sometimes when we really needed a decision his direction was non-existent. Nevertheless, he had great charisma and an indomitable sense of humor. And when the chips were really down he would hang in there with the rest of us—usually.

When the spacecraft went to Florida, we bade a fond farewell to our friends and lovers in LA and moved our flight crew operation to Florida also. We continued to spend some time in Houston for flight planning and other technical meetings, but the bulk of our activity took place at Cape Kennedy. We didn't get away from Florida very much because there was always some test or training exercise going on at the weekends. We were also swinging pretty good around Cocoa Beach.

Cocoa Beach and its vicinity happened to be the world's greatest astronaut fan club. Every move we made was chronicled and heralded by an instant-response grapevine net that covered and enmeshed the denizens of North Brevard County. Most of the folks there seemed to hold us in utmost awe, esteem, and affection and took keen interest in our affairs—romantic and otherwise. Their interest was understandable, since we were the hero-images of the space program on which many of them depended for their livelihood. Indeed, North Brevard fed and grew on governmental largesse through the expansion and flourishing of the space program at Kennedy Space Center for fifteen years—that is, until the bottom fell out.

I'm sure it is no surprise to anyone that among the residents there were a large number of attractive young ladies whose habit was to express their adulation of astronauts by sleeping with them. A good many were secretaries who were caught up in astro-hysteria at the Cape and at contractor offices in Cocoa Beach and the town of Cape Canaveral. Others were little chippies who worked as waitresses, telephone operators, and desk clerks around town. A few were young wives who were bored with their marriages and spent their evenings sitting around in the local bars, especially when astronauts were in town.

For the astronauts who played the game—and that included about three-fourths of those who had flown plus a great many others—these dalliances presented some rather interesting and unusual social situations. They practically lived in Cocoa Beach, their wives were in Houston, they had strong sexual compulsions, and enticing, eager females were readily available. They lived in constant dread of exposure because they believed it would be the ruination of their astronaut careers. Yet the fishbowl aspects of their existence in Florida almost guaranteed that their clandestine romantic romps would not go unnoticed. About the best they could hope for is that if they were properly circumspect and unobtrusive, the word wouldn't spread too far beyond Cocoa and, most important, wouldn't find its way into the newspapers.

The guys and their various girlfriends tended to congregate in a clandestine microcosm of society all their own. There were parties, dinners, beach romps, picnics, and weekend trips that were always held in seclusion and conducted in a vaguely furtive manner. Sometimes two or three couples got together in one of the guy's motel rooms for a few drinks and laughs, or on occasion for dining on fare from one of the local fast-food carry-out restaurants. Sometimes these little social affairs took place at someone's private home or apartment. But they rarely, if ever, took place in a public restaurant or nightspot. This had the added advantage of economy: a bottle of booze and a box of chicken were cheaper than drinks and dinner at a nice restaurant. Some of the worst rakes in the office were also the biggest tightwads.

Despite the abundance of available females locally, astronauts had been known to import girls from as far away as California. It must have taxed their ingenuity to keep the girls for days on end, and keep them happy, without spending a fortune or setting foot in public with them. One thing the guys had going for them was free—or nearly free—motel rooms. There were two motels at the Cape that catered to astronauts. The higher-priced one charged $1.50 a night, or $5 when guys had their wives along, which was rare. Girlfriends were not formally acknowledged and could stay with the guys for free. The other motel charged a dollar.

On a typical day the guys left for work about 7:30 a.m. and had breakfast and lunch in the crew quarters dining room, or sandwiches brought from the kitchen over to the simulator building. This left their lady guests to their own devices—and expenses—until the men returned late in the afternoon. For dinner they ate in the room on delicacies from the gourmet menu of Kentucky Fried or Fat Boy Bar-B-Q. Or they threw caution to the winds and drove fifty miles to a restaurant in Orlando or Vero Beach or Daytona and hoped no one saw them. For entertainment they might venture a drive-in movie, but more likely watched television and bedded down early. Infrequently they might wander into one of the local pubs with their ladies for a nightcap and a little dancing—but only in the late evening of a day early in a week comfortably distant from a launch date and after ascertaining that no newsmen or important visitors from Houston or Washington were in town. As far as I can see, all that the girls got out of this was the distinction of getting laid by an astronaut. And after all the years of all those astronauts running loose from one end of the country to the other, that wasn't much of a distinction.

It's curious how astronauts' sociosexual activities tended to run in tight little loops. They seemed to plow the same ground over and over. It could be quite ego-shattering for a guy to discover that his current flame had made it previously with one or more of his cohorts. In fact, he may find out that she was currently dallying with others of the group. However, the psychic trauma was usually minimal since the emotional involvement was normally nil. Once he got over the initial shock, the situation could be pretty funny. One astro-wag coined the term "Peters-in-law" to describe the quasi-incestuous circumstance where two or more astronauts had shared or were sharing the same woman. These adulterous activities ranged from one-night stands with strangers to deep involvements and serious love affairs over prolonged periods of months or even years. The latter were continuous—or intermittent.

Most astronauts' nocturnal enterprises lay somewhere between these two extremes. They tended to have casual intermittent affairs, perhaps several going on concurrently. No doubt their myriad female partners played the same game. This arrangement provided them with liberal amounts of sex of a great and fascinating variety. It also kept them off the streets and thus out of public scrutiny. And more to the point, it prevented them from wandering around until all hours, losing sleep and winding up empty-handed. Their polygamous behavior also tended to inhibit the formation of close entanglements with all the attendant complications, heartaches, and lingering aftermath. Nonetheless, serious relationships did evolve from time to time.

Naturally, some astronauts were more susceptible than others. One or two seemed to be in love continually with some broad or other. These affairs of course were more like adolescent infatuations—intense, erotic, but short-lived. Some guys had two or three really serious affairs that broke up in agony only when the guy's work took him elsewhere and circumstances precluded any further visits to his beloved. One of the troops had been going with the same girl for seven years, last I counted. He moved her all over the country so he could be with her. St. Louis, California, Florida—it must have been a hell of a life for both of them. He had a miserable marriage and two nice kids in Houston. I guess he was afraid to leave his wife for his girlfriend because it might have meant losing his position as one of the perennial space flyers. So he never told his wife and she pretended not to know—although everyone else did. Meanwhile, he kept his girlfriend hidden away. She found a little relief by having an occasional date or perhaps a brief affair with some other man.

We tried to spend weekends in Houston, but as launch day drew nearer we spent less and less time there, including weekends. We got busy as hell, trying to keep up with the work on the spacecraft. We were still a little skeptical and were dealing with an entirely new (to us) team of managers, engineers, and technicians, both contractor and NASA. Our training also intensified. We did a lot of work in our pressure suits, a time-consuming and sometimes fatiguing procedure. Then there was a succession of "flight sims," exercises where the spacecraft simulators in Florida were actually wired in to the Mission Control Center in Houston. The realism was incredible. You think for all the world that you're flying in space and talking with the controllers on the ground. It was just as real for them, too. Everything happened in "real time"—that is, in the same sequence and over the same time intervals that would occur during the actual flight.

I remember the way our rocket looked a couple of nights before launch. They had pulled back all the gantry structure and I could see it standing there, naked and stark white, bathed in the brilliance of high-intensity spotlights against a carbon black sky. And on top, the little white cone we would ride inside to orbit and inhabit for eleven long days. Some sight. I got goose bumps and "go fever" right then.

6. Liftoff

Ignition! We could feel the vibration and hear the deep-throated rumble as eight huge rocket engines came up to full thrust. The spacecraft shook and rattled furiously. I thought the Command Module was going to snap right off the top of that Saturn.

Liftoff! The clock is running! The instant the tie-downs released us, we could feel a lessening of vibrations and noise. There's no doubt about when liftoff occurs.

Bright orange flames burst forth from the base of the rocket. Great balls of black smoke billowed out and upward.

The whole ship vibrates and rattles. I think it's only the rocket exhaust plume hitting the launch structure, and the vibrations reflecting back into our Saturn rocket. But is that all it is? Is the rocket really okay?

I quickly scanned the instrument panel in front of me. I learned long ago as a young pilot to trust the instruments rather than a physical feeling or instinct. And sure enough, the instruments showed that everything was normal—and launch control confirmed, "The booster is looking good."

The Saturn stood still a few seconds, then slowly lifted away, trailing a stream of yellow fire. A deafening roar rolled across the flat wet marshes of the Cape. Two miles away where thousands of people gathered to watch, the ground shook and rumbled underfoot.

The toads, alligators, and crabs knew exactly what the noise and rumbling was all about. It was just another space shot. When you live at the Cape, you learn to live with this sort of thing. For years the humans had been sending things off into space. Yet even the Cape creatures probably knew that this was a big one.

Twenty seconds later, by the time we cleared the top of the launch gantry, all the shaking and rattling had smoothed out. The booster was tipping over now—that's called the pitch program. It *had* to tip over as we climbed so that it was flying level with the earth when we reached orbit.

As the rocket climbed higher, it tilted to the east. Out across the ocean it raced, gathering speed and growing smaller in the distance. Inside the spacecraft we watched the instruments and reported to mission control. Once in a while, when there was time, we talked to each other.

One minute after launch and we were going through the speed of sound, or Mach 1. There was a little rumbling and shaking again, but it only lasted a moment.

"Oh, boy!" I exclaimed. "That was some shaky ride for a while there, but it's pretty smoothed out now."

"Yeah," agreed Walt. "Pretty smooth now."

Now we were really starting to move. The force of the rocket thrust pushed us gently but firmly against the back of our seats. 2 g's, 3 g's, 4 g's— four times the force of gravity. The g-forces built up inexorably, mashing us harder and harder into our couches. But it felt comfortable and strangely reassuring, because we knew that the rocket was working, thrusting us faster and faster toward Earth orbit and outer space.

The forces built up to 4.5 g's, then *bam!* The first stage burned out abruptly and separated, and we were abruptly thrown forward into the straps of our restraint harnesses. We went weightless for a moment and it was all quiet. Then *bang!* A noise like a cannon shot and lights on the control panel told us the first stage had separated and was falling away, back toward Earth.

We would fall back to Earth, too, if the second stage didn't work right. We were traveling at nine thousand feet a second—about six thousand miles an hour. That's fast, but not fast enough for orbit.

A yellow light went out on the panel, the g-meter went from zero to half a g, and we were pushed gently back against our seats. All of this told us the second stage had ignited and started its thrusting. Then came a reassuring call from Mission Control—the second stage, or S-IVB, was "go."

A few seconds later, the booster inertial guidance system took over. The ship wiggled a little, then settled down again to the correct flight path, and we knew that booster guidance was "go."

We were coming up on three minutes from liftoff now, and it was time to jettison the launch escape tower, the big rocket at the very top of the spaceship that would pull the Command Module—and us with it—away from the rest of the ship if we'd had to abort the mission.

We were high enough and fast enough now that we didn't need the escape rocket anymore. And we had to get rid of it to continue the flight. If we didn't, the booster may have gone out of control before we reached orbit. Worse than that, the landing parachutes couldn't come out, and we absolutely had to have those parachutes for a safe landing at the end of the flight.

This was a moment of great tension for me as I glanced at the tower jettison switches and pondered the awful consequences of their *not* working. Either switch will do the job and there's not much chance they both won't work, but still—there's that nagging shred of doubt in your mind.

I threw the switches. There was a loud crack and a brief muffled roar, followed by a throaty, low-pitched whoosh as the escape rocket tower departed—and I heaved a great sigh of relief. We called Mission Control—"Tower jett."

They responded: "Roger, we confirm. Tower jett."

We were about four minutes into the flight now and we talked to Mission Control in Houston once a minute. We called in that the spacecraft guidance system was good and that all systems were go. Everything was going just beautifully, like clockwork. We were moving toward orbit, climbing and picking up speed all the time.

Our spacecraft guidance and navigation system was not controlling the booster—but it was sensing the motion and telling us where we were. Since I was the navigator on this flight, it was my job to keep track of our position and operate the guidance equipment. Right then I was reading our velocity and altitude off the computer, and I could see that we were right on the money.

Launch plus five minutes now, and we were halfway to orbit. There was not much to do for a while except watch the dials in front of us and talk to Mission Control once a minute—just to be sure they were still there.

For the first time I had a chance to look out the hatch window, just above my head. What a sight! What a view! I could see the most spectacular view of the whole Atlantic Ocean—hundreds and hundreds of miles of it—all deep blue and shimmering in the reflected sunlight of the noonday sun, with little patches of white puffy clouds dotting it here and there. And in the distance, toward the horizon, the blue gave way to a sort of faint purplish haze in the atmosphere. The sky above the far horizon was black as coal. It was just beautiful! I'd never seen anything like it. But then of course I'd never been this high before. I said something marvelously memorable like, "Boy, what a view!" It was pretty exciting. But at a time like that, words only serve to tarnish the pristine beauty of the moment.

In a few seconds the S-IVB rocket engine would stop—that's called cutoff—and we'd be in orbit. Our rate of climb was almost zero, which meant we were leveling off. The engine should shut down automatically, but we were ready to shut it off by manual control, if necessary.

Ready now? Standby—three, two, one, engine cutoff! We hit the straps again, but not as abruptly as the first time. I checked our computer and it said we had a good orbit, right on target. Mission Control gave us our orbit parameters based on radar tracking during launch. Spot on. I felt like ten million dollars. Altitude, 120 miles; rate of climb, zero; and velocity, 25,000 feet per second. Think of it! That's 17,000 miles an hour—fast enough to stay up in space and to circle the earth every ninety minutes.

Our spacecraft was still attached to the S-IVB, and we were sailing along upside down. Imagine that—we were over a hundred miles high and floating on our backs. But it didn't really matter, because we were weightless and there wasn't any sense or feeling of up or down.

I looked out at the world down below, and it was just zipping by. We were really hauling the freight. It was beautiful. By the end of that trip we'd make 163 revolutions of the earth. Aloft for 260 hours, we would see all of the world—literally every square mile of it—between the thirtieth parallels, north and south. It was awesome and breathtaking to see entire continents go whizzing past our windows in a matter of minutes. It was almost unreal—as if we were watching some giant relief map of the world, instead of the real earth itself going by.

But there was work to do. We stayed strapped in our couches until MCC, the Mission Control Center, gave us a go to proceed past the reentry point for the first revolution of the earth. Wally and Walt stayed strapped in until we received a go for three revolutions.

Mission Control called. "*Apollo 7*, this is Houston. We have a 'go' for the third orbit. I repeat, you are cleared for three orbits. Acknowledge. Over."

"Roger, Houston," answered Wally. "Understand, we are 'go' for three orbits."

First I removed my helmet and gloves and handed them to Walt and Wally. The cabin was quiet and peaceful now that the rocket had shut off. All I could hear was the soft whirr of some electrical equipment. Then I released my lap belt and floated slowly out of my seat—my first real test of weightlessness.

I'm free! I'm floating! What a feeling! It was a little strange at first, and my muscles were tense. I had a mild but disconcerting feeling of vague apprehension for a few minutes, and my head and face felt flushed, full, and stuffy.

But this feeling of being utterly free of gravity was simply beautiful— and after a few minutes it was no longer strange but very comfortable, and I could feel my muscles relax. The apprehension went away quickly, but the stuffiness persisted throughout the flight.

Wally and Walt got loose, took off their gloves and helmets, and gave them to me. My first chore was to stow them, and other loose items. I folded down the leg rests of my crew couch and pulled myself ever so slowly into the lower equipment bay of the spacecraft, easing myself feet first. I moved slowly to keep from bumping into things, plus the feeling of floating and turning felt strange and a little scary at first. I put them away along with my own, in a large bag under the center couch.

There were plenty of storage lockers, retaining straps, and elastic cords— and Velcro to stick things to the walls. I opened some metal boxes that were fastened to the floor and took out a camera bracket, a box of tissues, some books, and a special control box with a long cable. I put the books in the pockets of my space suit and gave the rest of the stuff to Walt and Wally. Then I floated slowly beneath the couches again and took out three long white bags. I gave one to Wally, another to Walt, and snapped the other onto the cabin wall. The bags were made of fireproof cloth with elastic around the top to hold them shut. We would use the bags to put things in—cameras, pencils, books, food bags, anything that might otherwise float away and get lost.

Everything had to be tied down or put away, or else we would have had objects floating all over the spacecraft. But it was no trouble, really, and in a very short time we fell quite naturally into the routine of housekeeping. Once in a while, though, something got away from us—a food bag, a pen, or a flashlight—and disappeared for a while. I once lost a checklist—I looked all over the spacecraft and couldn't find it. About an hour later it reappeared, drifting slowly across the lower equipment bay.

There were plenty of things to hold onto to pull myself about when I wanted to move. The braces that held our couches, drawer latches, and hatch handles—any little knob or other object sticking out—would serve as a foothold or handgrip.

Being weightless was really a lot of fun. I was beginning to think that it is mankind's natural state—that everybody ought to experience the delights of zero-g. It seemed a pity that everyone in the world but the three of us had to be plastered down against the earth by the force of gravity.

We were flying upside down on the forward end of the second stage, with Walt and Wally's heads pointed toward Earth. But "up" and "down" have little meaning in space, and the two spacemen hardly noticed the inverted position. True, the angle of view was peculiar, but viewing the earth from far out in space is unusual from any angle. This attitude gave us a fantastic view of the earth through all five windows. Walt and Wally, still strapped in their seats, could look upward at an angle through the front windows and see the earth rolling by: oceans dark blue and shimmering in reflected sunlight, turning pale green in the shallows near islands and coastlines; white cotton puffs of clouds; the dark-green blankets that were jungles and forests; and beige-tinted desert sands in rippling waves of dunes, almost like the sea.

Walt looked out the side window by his right elbow. He saw nothing but black, the stark black emptiness of outer space. Walt knew the stars were out there, but he couldn't see them because the spacecraft was still in daylight.

"How do you like the ride, Walt?" asked Wally, his face all crinkly with a smile.

"Swell," replied Walt as he loosened his seat belt and shoulder harness. "What a gorgeous view—wish we had more time to look," he added as he gazed through the window at the earth.

"Yeah, so do I," said Wally, "but let's get our work done first. We will have time for sightseeing later. Right now we have to get ready for separation."

The navigation system optics pointed upward toward the sky and afforded an unobstructed view of the stars. We were still in daylight when I moved the optics controls to pop off the launch protective cover.

Wally looked at his watch and at the timer on the panel in front of him. The seconds were ticking away. "Hey, Donn," he called, "better shake a leg. Ten minutes 'til sunset."

"Okay, Wally," I responded. "I'll pop the optics cover. Hope it comes off all right."

"Yeah, it will be tough to navigate if we can't see out through the sextant," Walt chimed in. A round plate covered the outer lenses of a telescope and sextant built into the side of the ship. The plate protected those instruments during launch, but to use them for star sightings I had to get rid of the cover plate. I looked into the telescope eyepiece and saw nothing but black. I pushed a small lever and—*boingg!*

"Wow! That's spectacular!" I exclaimed.

"Did it come off okay? What do you see?" asked Walt excitedly.

"It popped right out there," I answered. "I can still see the plate, drifting away slowly, wobbling and settling. Looks like a tin can lid sinking in water."

I saw the cover through the telescope, light-bulb-bright in reflected sunlight against the black void of space, undulating in slow motion and floating eerily away, like a jar lid might move and settle under water.

"What color is it?" asked Wally.

"No special color," I replied. "Just brilliant shining white in the sun. And there must be thousands of tiny snowflakes."

A cloud of particles that looked like snowflakes made seeing the stars impossible. We had been wise in planning to do our star sightings on the dark side of the earth, where stray light would not obliterate our view of the heavens.

"Those are probably dust particles that shook loose when the cover plate popped off," explained Wally. "The sun is so bright up here it makes them look like snow." He had seen them before, on his other spaceflights.

"I can't stand the suspense," announced Walt. "I've got to see this." And with that, he unbuckled his harness and floated toward the optics panel, taking care not to tangle himself in the suit hoses.

"Oh, sob," moaned Wally. "Just what we need. A couple of spaced-out sightseers."

"Get him," said Walt, jerking his thumb toward Wally. "He's just sore because he didn't think of it first."

"Well, Walt, you know how it is. As you get older you lose your enthusiasm," I declared, moving aside to let Walt peer through the 'scope. I glanced sideways to see if Wally would react to this remark. Wally was a little older than us two, and he didn't like to be reminded of it.

"All right, you turkeys, out of the way!" ordered Wally, sounding very stern. "I'm coming down there."

"Hey, wait!" I protested. "There isn't room for all three of us down here.

Wait till I get out of the way. Besides, who is going to watch the instrument panel?"

"The instrument panel is your problem," snorted Wally as he unbuckled and started drifting down. I scurried to get out of the way but my hoses became tangled. As Wally came gliding in, he jammed himself next to me into the left corner of the lower bay area. Walt, in the center with his eye glued to the telescope, didn't even notice.

"Hey, Walt, move over, will you? I'm stuck," I pleaded.

"Huh?" said Walt, looking to his left and then laughing.

Wally looked through the telescope but didn't see any of the snowflakes. Walt and I exchanged wide-eyed, baffled glances. How could he not have seen all those brilliant flakes? And then it dawned on Walt.

"Wait a minute," he exclaimed. "No wonder. We just passed sunset. No more daylight!"

And sure enough, as we looked out the spacecraft windows, we saw not the bright earth but only darkness.

"I hope you can see some stars," I commented.

"Yes, I can make out a few of the brighter ones," announced Wally. "Should be good enough to navigate by."

"Good, how about letting me take a crack at it?" I asked.

"She's all yours," said Wally as he drifted away and back to his seat.

I grabbed the couch struts and slowly pulled myself toward the optics panel. I came slowly to a stop with my eye against the telescope. The stars were hard to see at first, but as my eye got used to the darkness I could see more and more. Finally, the familiar patterns of constellations began to appear—Orion the hunter; Taurus the bull; and the Gemini twins. And with those patterns I could spot several "Apollo" stars. Of all the thousands of stars in the heavens, thirty-eight had been picked to use with the Apollo guidance computer. I knew if I used any others the computer would get confused and line up the guidance system wrong.

"*Apollo 7*, Houston here, over."

"Roger Houston, Seven here," answered Wally.

"The flight director advises, proceed with imu alignment. We're monitoring your computer readings," advised capcom.

"How about that?" I said, checking first to be sure my microphone was turned off. "The very first alignment, and I've got an audience already."

"What do you mean?" asked Walt.

"Everything I do shows up on the computer and gets telemetered back to Houston," I explained.

"Oh, that's right," Walt said. After a moment's thought he added, "Well, I hope they enjoy the show."

The inertial instrument unit, or IMU, measured changes in the ship's velocity and kept track of which way it pointed in space. And the IMU had to be lined up right with the stars by use of a sextant, an instrument much like a telescope that could be used to see stars and measure angles. I worked swiftly through the alignment sequence, driving the sextant to point toward one star and then another. I used a tiny control stick, the size of my little finger, which was mounted on the optics panel near the sextant. Each time I centered the sextant on a star I pressed the "Mark" button. That told the computer to measure the sextant angles.

The computer figured out how much the inertial unit had drifted from where it should be pointing, and drove the unit back to the correct position by sending small pulses to tiny electric motors. The IMU was only off by one degree, but it was important to get it lined up just right. I succeeded in getting a good platform alignment with star sightings on the second revolution. We went through some systems checks and got ready to separate from the second stage.

The three of us worked like beavers. Walt engrossed himself in checking the instruments on the panel in front of him: propellant temperatures, oxygen pressure, and battery voltage. Wally talked at length to Mission Control. I stood in the lower equipment bay. Or rather, I floated, since I was weightless like everything else in the spacecraft. But staying put wasn't too hard, I discovered. The stiff white air hoses attached to my space suit tended to hold me still in one place. And the suit was so large and bulky that there wasn't much room to move around anyway.

All the measurements of our spaceship systems—pressures, temperatures, and so on—were sent to Mission Control and they could tell better than we could what shape our craft was in. There were hundreds of those measurements and we could read only a small part of our spacecraft. Those guys could really do a job for us—if anything started to go wrong, they would know about it sooner than we would—and they would have a procedure worked out to get us around the problem.

As spaceflights go, ours was in a pretty low orbit—that was so we could get down in a hurry if we had to. But we were out of contact with Mission Control a lot of the time. So it was up to the three of us to keep an eye on our instruments and to know our emergency procedures: even to reenter and land on our own if we had to. And it was the training *before* the flight—all those hundreds of hours in simulators, and studying checklists and emergency procedures, which really goes to work for you up there in orbit. Up there, it was just the three of us and our spacecraft—and the skill and experience from all that training that stood between success or failure. Our training made it possible for us to do that job, make the flight that thousands of people in dozens of different places all worked hard for years to prepare for. That flight, *Apollo 7*, the maiden voyage of Apollo, was the payoff—for us and for them. And for all the millions of people in our country and around the world who were rooting for us, praying, and cheering us on. That is what it was all about for the three of us then.

We finished all our systems checks—*Apollo 7* was in great shape. Mission Control cleared us to separate. It was a simple procedure, but we went through it step by step using our checklist just to be sure we did it all in the right order. We did everything by checklist, even though we knew it all by heart. We'd throw a switch to ignite an explosive charge. The charge was shaped to cut the metal skin holding our spacecraft and the rocket stage together.

Time passed slowly for us as we waited for the exact minute to separate *Apollo 7* from the rocket stage. We were once again strapped snug in our seats, with all the right switches in the correct position and ready for separation.

"*Apollo 7*, Houston here. Five minutes to separate. Please confirm." The hollow-sounding voice of capcom crackling in our headsets interrupted our reveries, for we were all strangely quiet, each alone in our private thoughts.

"Roger, Houston, we're ready," affirmed Wally. "Five minutes, the timer is counting."

He sat comfortably in the left crew couch, the flight instruments and maneuvering controls before him. I watched the computer carefully as it blinked and flashed its eerie green-colored numbers. Walt kept an eye on the instruments in front of him. The time passed in painful slowness as the tension built up.

Until finally—"*Apollo 7*, Houston here counting down to separation.

Ten . . . nine . . . eight . . ." Capcom counted the last few seconds. "Two . . . one . . . separate!" At that instant Wally pushed forward on the T-shaped thruster, and I flipped the separation switches.

A loud crack like a rifle shot resounded through the ship as a small explosive charge cut us loose. The ring-shaped explosive charge had done its work and cut the spacecraft free from the booster. A soft muffled "whoosh" told us the thrusters were working, and the computer clicked off the small changes in speed as *Apollo 7*, free at last, moved away from the huge s-iv b rocket.

"Boy, that was some crack!" exclaimed Walt. "Sounded like the whole rear end exploded."

We thrusted away slowly using our small reaction control rockets. The booster was behind us and we couldn't see it, so I had the computer running to tell us how fast we were moving away.

The ship drifted slowly forward. At exactly sixty seconds after separating, Wally began to turn the ship around. He used a small control stick called the attitude controller to point the ship in the right direction. The little thruster rockets on the outside of *Apollo 7* went *ffft! ffft!* as they fired in short pulses, slowly pitching the spacecraft through a half somersault to face the s-iv b.

We turned around so we could see the booster, then used our reaction rockets to stop drifting away and move in close.

"Beautiful! Beautiful!" Walt cried out.

"Okay, Walt, can you see it?" asked Wally with excitement. "Get the camera ready and take some shots as I move in close."

The s-iv b loomed large and awesome in the front windows as Wally maneuvered closer. It looked like a large black and white tin can, about twenty feet across and sixty feet long. On the end facing us were four large tapered panels partly spread like petals on a flower, which had opened when we left it. The whole thing looked like a giant four jawed garfish, or some giant whale waiting to swallow us up if we got too close.

"Look at that!" I exclaimed. "A giant squid in the sky!"

"Or a crocodile with four nasty jaws," offered Walt. "Don't get too close, Wally. The darn thing might eat us."

Wally glanced over at his crewmates and shook his head. "Tsk, tsk. Just like a couple of kids at a carnival," he smirked. "What imaginations!"

We went in close anyway, to get a good look and take some pictures. We all enjoyed looking at the booster from different angles as Wally flew the craft smoothly around the s-ivb. We reported what we saw to Mission Control.

It was time to leave our booster now. "Houston, *Apollo 7*," I called, speaking through the small, stick-shaped microphone attached to my headset. "Have you got our attitude angles for the phasing maneuver?"

"Roger, Seven," came back the metallic voice of capcom. "Here they are. Ready to copy?"

"Affirmative. Go ahead," I answered.

"Okay. Pitch, zero three eight . . . Roll, two two seven . . . Yaw, three five two. Read back, please."

I read the numbers back, to be sure I had gotten them right.

"Okay, you've got them," reported capcom. "Also, your delta v is minus x, seven feet per second."

"Roger, Houston, delta v minus x seven feet per second," I acknowledged. That meant the spacecraft, when it was lined up in the right direction, should thrust backward seven feet a second, or about four miles an hour. This small change in velocity would be enough to make *Apollo 7* drift hundreds of miles away from the s-ivb.

Walt and I floated loose in our straps as Wally steered the ship around to the correct angle. I punched some numbers on the computer's keyboard that told it to measure the change in speed. At just the right moment, Wally pulled back on the T-shaped thruster control. The thrusters made their soft whooshing sound again as *Apollo 7* slowly backed away from the s-ivb.

"Goodbye, old friend," called Walt as the receding s-ivb got smaller and smaller. "See you tomorrow." And then, "I hope," he added wistfully.

"What do you mean, you hope?" I huffed. "Are you suggesting we might not make the rendezvous?"

"Listen, without any radar on this ship I'd say the rendezvous is at best an even bet. We may make it, we may not," asserted Wally.

"Oh, ye of little faith," I groaned.

"Who is little Faith?" taunted Walt. "I haven't met her."

"If you don't thtop making joketh, I'll thlap *your* fathe," joked Wally.

"Oh, boy!" I moaned.

Wally burst out laughing. "Hah! That's your first 'Oh boy' since lift-off," referring to the fact that I was given to saying "Oh, boy" whenever Wally cracked a corny pun, which was pretty often.

"Anyway, we'll be joining up again with the s-ivb tomorrow. And I say we'll make the rendezvous, radar or no radar. I've got a feeling in my bones." Wally patted the computer. "Old Nellie here won't let us down."

As *Apollo 7* drifted on, Wally watched the s-ivb shrink to a dot of bright light while Walt switched inverters and checked main electrical system voltages. I floated casually in the lower bay area of the spacecraft's cabin, gazing through the telescope at the earth below. A range of rough, rugged mountains in east Africa passed below. The sun was setting there, and from my vantage point one hundred and fifty miles above I could see the tall lavender-streaked peaks casting crazy-quilt patterns of long shadows over the broken, rumpled landscape. As we sped eastward the shades of lavender and pink faded to dull gray as the shadows softened, blurred and finally blended with the gray. And the gray quickly deepened into the blackness of night.

"Lovely, lovely," I exclaimed.

"What's lovely?" inquired Walt.

"The earth," I replied. "A mountain sunset, from this angle, is really something to behold."

"Sorry I missed it," sighed Walt, disappointed.

"Don't sweat it, Walt," interjected Wally. "If this machine holds together like it's supposed to, we'll have a hundred and sixty more sunsets just like that one. You're bound to see your share."

"Yeah, I guess you're right," agreed Walt. "It's hard to realize that we go all the way around the earth in ninety minutes. Think of that—a sunrise and sunset every hour and a half."

"*Apollo 7*, Houston, over," called the voice of Mission Control in our headsets.

"Roger, Houston, go ahead," answered Wally.

"Seven, the flight director advises you are cleared to doff your suits anytime you want."

"Okay, thanks, Houston. I think we'll doff suits right now," Wally replied as Walt and I nodded vigorously in agreement.

"It will sure be nice to get out of this hot, lumpy thing," Walt remarked.

"You're right," I said. "And since I'm supposed to go first, how about helping me with this zipper?"

Because there were too many fittings and gadgets in the front, the large, cumbersome pressure suit had been built with its zipper in back. The wearer required the help of another person to zip and unzip.

The space suit was made entirely in one piece except for the gloves and the plastic bubble helmet, which fastened into metal rings at the wrists and neck. To put it on or take it off, we had to wriggle in and out through the full-length zipper opening in the back.

The suits protected us from the vacuum of space by keeping a blanket of air circulating inside. Astronauts on other missions wore these protective garments whenever they went for a walk in space or on the moon. And they wore them during launch from the Cape to guard against a loss of air from the cabin—an unlikely but possible happening. But *Apollo 7* had been aloft for several hours now, and since everything on the ship seemed to be in good working order, the flight director had decided it was safe for us to take off the suits.

I glided from my usual position in the center couch to the equipment bay, where there was more room to move about. Drifting freely in mid-space I crouched, bent double, tucked in my chin, and pulled the suit's neck ring over my head. Working free of the suit's rubbery arms and legs, I folded the bulky garment carefully and stuffed it into a large white cloth bag beneath the center couch.

"Okay, Walt, it's your turn," I called as I slid out of the equipment bay to make room for my crewmate. Walt slithered out of his pressure suit with ease, quickly folded it, and placed the suit in the bag next to mine.

Wally, of stockier build and less flexible than his two companions, encountered some difficulty in extracting himself from his suit. He bent double and tucked in his chin, but could not compress himself enough for the neck ring to pass over the back of his head. "Help, somebody!" Wally cried, his voice muffled and his face buried inside the suit. "Give me a hand, will you?"

"Whatever you say," said Walt agreeably, and began clapping his hands in applause.

"Not that kind of a hand, you knothead," said Wally laughing at himself for the absurd posture into which he had gotten himself.

"Let me see if I can get you out of there," I said. I grasped the neck ring, pulled it toward me, and pushed down on Wally's head. I puffed and Wally grunted as we struggled with the suit. Together we managed to stretch it enough for Wally to pull his head past the neck ring and pop out through the zipper opening.

"Hello there!" I said. "We've been waiting for you."

"Just like a butterfly coming out of its cocoon," Walt observed.

"I'm just so proud to be here!" quipped Wally, shucking off the arms and legs of his space suit.

Wally put his suit away with Walt's and mine. From a small compartment he withdrew three sets of jackets and trousers, the coveralls we would wear throughout most of the flight. The coveralls were made of a special fireproof Teflon cloth which felt clammy and slick to the touch.

"Try these on," offered Wally. "They're just what the well-dressed spaceman will wear."

"Oh boy!" I exclaimed with mock enthusiasm. "The latest style in men's spacey sportswear."

"Well, don't knock it," said Walt. "Sure beats those hot, lumpy things we just took off."

We were supposed to stay up there for eleven days, but our flight was planned so that we could come down early if anything went wrong. Most of our tests were scheduled for the first two days, so that if we had to cut the mission short we could still complete most of our tests. But what we were really trying to do was prove that the Apollo spaceship design was flight-worthy to make trips to the moon and back—on later missions— and we had to keep it running for eleven days to do that.

The mission was going along very well and we were right on schedule. Our flight plan was carefully worked out so that we could make the most of our hours in space. We had to find out all we could about that spacecraft because the mission plans for later flights depended a lot on what happened and how we got along on this one.

The next few hours passed almost without notice as we busied ourselves with dozens of checks, tests, and inspections of the spaceship and all its equipment. *Apollo 7* was a brand-new ship, the very first of its kind to fly in space. Some day, a craft just like this one would carry humans to the moon—if, that is, all went well on this first, maiden voyage of Apollo. There was much to be learned about the ways Apollo and all its different systems performed during flight through space.

Our daily schedule was set up for someone to be awake all the time, so we took turns sleeping. For eight hours every day I was awake by myself, while my crewmates slept. I expected to be bored and lonely, but somehow I was not. There was always something to do: clean up the cabin, write in the log book, eat, take pictures, and talk to my friends at Mission Control. And I enjoyed the quiet hours, the peace and tranquility; it allowed me a chance to think about how I got to be there—ponder what it all meant, reflect on the silent beauty of the earth going by—or gaze out at the stars, so clear and bright in the infinite blackness of space beyond Earth. I'm kind of a loner, and I like quiet times.

I was supposed to go to sleep at six o'clock Eastern time. I unrolled my sleeping bag under Walt's couch and crawled in. But who the hell can go to sleep at 6:00 p.m. the first day in space? Not me. I might as well have been sitting on my head on top of a flag pole. It was the wrong time of day, and I was still exhilarated by the experiences of the past few hours. In fact, I had trouble sleeping the whole time we were up there, on account of the weird hours of my sleep schedule and Walt and Wally's activities and conversation. That first night I spent more time looking over Walt's shoulder at the instruments (our sleeping bags were slung beneath the left and right couches) than I did sleeping. Every now and then he would turn around expecting to see me asleep, and instead he found himself staring into two beady eyes. I was preoccupied with thinking about the rendezvous coming up the next day. After that night I'd get by on catnaps for two days and collapse every third night for a solid six to eight hours.

"Well, I'm glad we're through with all of that," sighed Wally as we finished the last of our long list of checks and tests.

"Yeah, so am I," said Walt. "I'm really tired," he added, yawning and stretching. "Is it time to turn in yet?"

"Just about," I replied. "Why don't you go on and get some sleep? It's been a long day. There is nothing left to do that I can't manage on my own."

"Yes, I think you're right," said Wally. "Come on, Walt, let's hit the sack. Donn, keep an eye on things. If anything important happens, be sure to wake me up."

"Right, Wally. Don't worry, I will," I responded.

Walt and Wally slipped beneath their couches, where sleeping bags hung suspended by straps attached to opposite walls. The two men unzipped the thin cloth bags and snuggled themselves inside.

"Good night, all," Walt called out.

"Pleasant dreams," I said.

Wally didn't say anything, but he moaned contentedly as he got himself into a comfortable position and promptly went off to sleep. Walt at first missed the familiar, comforting feeling of a mattress pressing against his body. But the strange new feeling of floating while trying to rest soon gave way to weariness, and in a very few minutes Walt, too, fell fast asleep.

I had work to do while Wally and Walt were sleeping. One thing was taking pictures of the earth. That's pretty important. Photographs taken at that altitude show a lot of things about the earth that people just can't see when they are right down on the surface. Down there, you can't see the forest for the trees. I reached down into one of the long white storage bags and took out a box-shaped camera. Stowing the lens cover so it wouldn't float all over the cabin, I snapped some pictures.

I always powered up the guidance system in the computer to prepare for the next day during my night watch. I did it one orbit earlier than the flight plan asked for, so it would all be ready when Walt and Wally woke up, and they would not have to rush. I also liked to align the platform using no fuel, and sometimes I could fly an entire orbit and not see any stars because *Apollo 7* was tipped at the wrong angle. If I started early on a dark pass with a spacecraft attitude where I could see stars, I could align without using fuel.

We found a number of times in the flight where we could perform tests in a more effective and efficient way than the flight plan called for. Conserving fuel was very important, because we always wanted to keep a little in reserve as a backup for when we deorbited, in case we lost our thrusters. We didn't have fuel gauges, so had to rely on the ground to tell us how much fuel they believed we had left.

"Talking to yourself again, Donn?" grumped Wally one morning, unzipping his sleeping bag and floating feet first from under his couch.

"Huh?" I grunted, startled. "Ah, no. I think I was singing 'Show Me the Way to Go Home.'"

"You *are* home," quipped Walt, swinging a snappy half-somersault feet first over the end of his couch. "And the next line to that song is 'I'm tired and I want to go to bed.'"

"Yeah. So go, man," ordered Wally. "To bed, that is. Pretty good sleeping, I might add. Once you get used to not having a bed under you."

"Yeah, that is a little weird," echoed Walt. "Anything happen while we were sleeping?"

"No, nothing special. Everything is normal," I answered. "I did all the checks as scheduled. You will find all the readings and results in the crew log. Got a couple of flight plan updates from Mission Control. Wrote them down in the plan. Any more questions?"

"No, guess not," groaned Walt, stretching and yawning.

I floated down beneath the couches and wriggled into my sleeping bag. "Good night, you guys," I called out.

7. Rendezvous

The second day of the flight was the toughest and busiest up there. We had to rendezvous with the booster. This was the high point of the mission for me, since I was the navigator and chief computer operator and had the most to do with getting us back to the second stage. What made it tough was that we had no radar on board to measure distance and closing speed to the target. It was all done through optical sightings and computer calculations. Of course, we had a lot of help from Mission Control in setting up the initial conditions. They had good radar track on both us and the target. But after we started the transfer maneuver it was all on board and up to us—which meant up to me, mostly.

That computer had a personality, however. It got smart-aleck over some landmark tracking, for example, when updating our position and velocity in relation to the earth. For a while, it kept telling me that one of our landmarks, a well-surveyed airport or peninsula, was 3,500 feet underwater. I thought it had a lot of nerve, trying to correct the cartographers like that.

We had a pretty good system worked out. I took charge and made decisions, operated the computer, and made the optical sightings on the target. Walt sat on the right and kept an eye on the other spacecraft systems and worked the backup rendezvous charts that could give us some answers we needed to make the rendezvous in case the computer crapped out. Wally sat on the left and did the manual maneuvering—a lot of it was automatic—and kibitzed.

The flight was going along butter smooth, and all of our equipment was working normally. And it was a good thing, because we would need everything we had to pull the rendezvous off.

We were going to rejoin our booster stage because we wanted to prove that on later flights the command ship could rescue the Lunar Module if it had to, if it couldn't rendezvous for some reason. Of course on those flights, both ships had radar. We didn't have radar, and without it, rendezvous in space was a pretty tricky deal. But we rehearsed it many times in the simulators, and I was sure we could do it.

We had a couple of hurdles to get over. The first one was to power up the guidance system and align the inertial measurement unit, or IMU, that we used to keep track of our directions and position in space. We'd turned off the whole system several hours earlier, to save electric power. Since then we had not had any control of our attitude—we had been rolling and tumbling, tilting at any old angle as we drifted along through space.

To align the IMU I had to measure angles between stars with the sextant and telescope built into the side of our ship. We had to be on the dark side of the earth; there was too much light on the sun side to see the stars. And the spacecraft had to be tipped the right way for me to see the sky through the telescope instead of the ground below us. I could turn on the control rockets to stop the motion, but I didn't want to use them any more than necessary. We were trying to save rocket fuel, too.

The other hurdle was our main rocket engine. It had never been fired except on a test stand, on the ground, long before it was installed in the spacecraft. And we had to fire it twice to set up the rendezvous. We were not really worried about it—there was not much chance it wouldn't work—but since this was the first time we wanted to be on our toes in case anything went haywire. For example, if the engine gimbal went hard over and we didn't catch it right away, the ship would spin up like a top. That might not be disastrous, but it sure could ruin the day for us. If the main rocket engine didn't start, or if it blew up, we would have to come down right away and use our emergency deorbit procedures. And if the rocket didn't stop on time, we might end up in some weird orbit that would be hard to get out of.

We set up to do the first burn—we did it under computer control and punched in all the right numbers. We had a "go" from Mission Control and we sat strapped in our seats with arms folded, watching the instruments and the computer display as it counted down to ignition time . . .

T minus twenty seconds and we thrust forward with the small control rockets. We heard gurgling sounds as main rocket fuel sloshed and settled to the bottom of the tanks.

Three, two, one, ignition! And *bam!* We were thrown against the back of our seats by the sudden onset of thrust. We had been weightless for a day, and the sudden feeling of the equivalent of earth's gravity slapping me in the back was startling. It felt like a steamroller was running over me. What a sensation! It was like that big jug was driving us straight for the moon. I felt like I was along for the ride, and I hoped it would shut off when it was supposed to. Then, abruptly, the thrusting stopped and we were thrown forward against our shoulder harnesses. It only lasted ten seconds, but what a kick in the back it was! And I made a mental note to myself, next time, to strap in a little tighter.

Our first rocket burn was a good one, according to the computer, and Mission Control confirmed our results. They were tracking us on radar from the ground. They were also tracking our s-ivb target and computing our flight path to the final approach to rendezvous. Thanks to them, we were sliding right up the pipe.

The next thing was the transfer maneuver that would carry us up to the higher orbit of our target. After that it was all on board because the ground couldn't help us anymore. We had to do it all ourselves.

To track the target, I used the telescope and sextant, which were tied to the computer. I had to measure the angle to the target and let the computer calculate when, in what direction, and how much thrust to apply to reach the target. We did the thrusting here with the small reaction control rockets, not the big one. It was a little like joining up two airplanes, except it was all backward—to catch up you slow down, to fall behind you speed up. You know it's all based on laws of physics, but it still seemed weird.

I had an unwelcome surprise. The computer took around four minutes to think over its solution for the transfer burn. In the simulator, it had also continued to track the target. But here in space, it stopped tracking when I had to change from one computer program to another. I didn't worry, thinking I could pick it up again in our telescope.

About fifteen minutes before the critical transfer burn, the computer finally finished its computation, and I had something of a crisis. I had been making sightings on the flashing light affixed to our target. But now I had lost sight of the target completely—we were in total darkness, and the target's tracking light was too dim to show up in the telescope. The sextant had a narrow field of view, and once it got off target I couldn't find it.

Wally couldn't see it out of the window either. It was pretty traumatic for us. What we had to do now was rely on the computer and hope it was right. The numbers we were getting looked good. I decided to go ahead with the transfer burn, since successive computer solutions for it had converged and tallied pretty well with Walt's results from the backup charts. Afterward, perhaps, we could reacquire the target. Maybe by then we would be close enough to see the light in the telescope.

We did the burn, recycled the computer into the next program, and it worked! It worked! The burn went okay and we appeared to be on the proper track to the target. I found the flashing light again, with the help of the computer, and resumed tracking. We were preparing for the first midcourse correction when Wally started hollering for a floodlight shield to keep the light from reflecting in his eyes and blinding him while he was trying to look out of the front window.

In the ensuing scramble for the light shield, I lost my checklist. Somehow in all the confusion it got loose and drifted off. In looking for the checklist, I got behind in the rendezvous sequence and missed some measurements and calculations. There was a pretty frantic free-for-all in the cockpit for a while. But I found it again, beneath my couch—just in time to do the midcourse correction. It turned out great, and we slid right up the pipe to the target. It was a great feeling.

During the final phase—the last mile or two—it was pretty much on Wally. All the maneuvers and corrections were manual and the measurements by eyeball out the front window as the rocket stage loomed larger and larger. If he came in too fast we'd whistle on by. If he came in too slow we'd stall out and never get there.

We were in daylight from about two miles on in, and we got our first good look at the target. Look at that monster—we were really getting in close!

When we got within a mile of the target, Wally was supposed to estimate by eyeball the remaining distance, since the computer's accuracy degraded at close ranges. With less than a mile to go, the computer wasn't much help anymore. Without radar, we had to judge our distance and closing rate by eyeball, according to how big the target looked. We had a scheme to help Wally by use of a chart or target's subtended angle (measured visually) versus distance. For some reason Wally was reluctant to do this, and kept asking me for range-to-go readings off the computer. It was strange that he

1. Practicing ocean recovery techniques in 1966.

2. The *Apollo 7* crew a few months before launch.

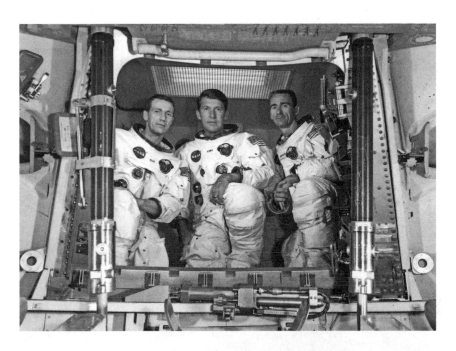

3. (*Opposite*) At the North
American plant in Downey,
California.

4. (*Above*) The crew through
the Apollo spacecraft hatch.

5. (*Right*) A smiling Donn
Eisele during space suit testing.

6. The Command and Service Modules that made up the *Apollo 7* spacecraft.

7. Crew press conference a few weeks before launch.

8. Training in the spacecraft simulators in the days before launch.

9. Training in the days prior to launch.

10. Briefing in the crew quarters by Deke Slayton two days before launch.

11. Reading over the flight plan two days before launch.

12. The rocket the day before launch.

13. Donn Eisele reads the morning paper before launch.

14. Donn Eisele at the pre-launch breakfast. Note his mug with "What's His Name" written on it.

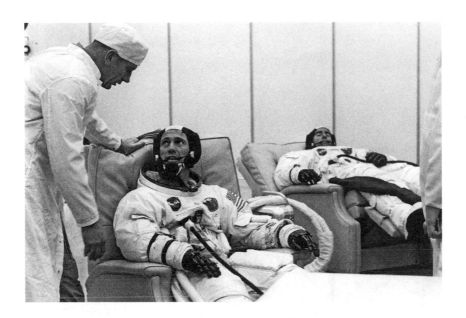

15. Some final words from Deke Slayton to Donn Eisele before launch.

16. Preparing to launch into space.

17. Donn Eisele and Walt Cunningham on launch morning.

18. *Apollo 7* launches into higher-than-planned winds.

19. *Apollo 7* clears the top of the launch gantry.

20. *Apollo 7* accelerates into space.

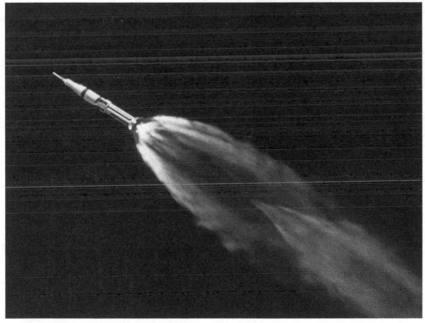

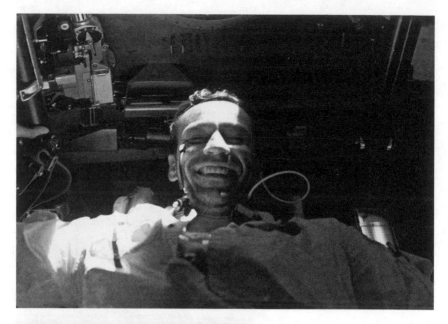

21. A happy Donn Eisele in space.

22. Donn Eisele caught in the sun's glare in space.

23. Film still of Donn Eisele working in space.

24. Rendezvous with the booster in orbit.

25. Flying close to the
s-ivb booster in space.

26. Donn Eisele in space, with the sextant behind him.

27. Donn Eisele and Wally Schirra during the TV show from space.

28. Arriving on the deck of the recovery carrier.

29. The crew escorted along the red carpet under stormy skies after splashdown.

30. A nauseous Donn Eisele soon after returning to Earth.

31. Taking a phone call from President Johnson.

32. The *Apollo 7* spacecraft is recovered from the ocean.

33. On the recovery ship after a shower, shave, and change of clothes.

34. The crew returns to the launch site in triumph.

35. Extensive debriefings after the mission.

36. With Deke Slayton after the flight.

37. Receiving an award from President Johnson.

was skeptical of the computer, yet perversely insisted on relying on it when its calculations were the least reliable.

I think his behavior reflected an insecurity and lack of confidence about the rendezvous and his ability to complete it without the crutch of radar data to lean on. And of course if it didn't work out, he would need something—or someone—to blame it on. The computer would have made an excellent scapegoat.

Actually, Walt and I shared his uneasiness about doing rendezvous without the benefit of radar. That's why we spent so much time on it in the simulator and tried—unsuccessfully—to get Wally to do it. We knew it was a tough job but figured that with lots of practice, and assuming no equipment failures and a reasonable initial setup from Mission Control's radar data, we could do it with reasonable facility.

Wally could see the rocket stage, but I couldn't see it from the middle seat. He yelled at me to tell him how far away we were. I refused, because I didn't believe the computer's numbers anymore. "If you tell me how big the booster looks," I told him, "I'll tell you how far away we are." We argued back and forth about whose job it was to decide how far away we were.

Quarter mile, one hundred yards, one hundred feet, and stop! We made it! We're here! Despite the difficulties, Wally had milked it in to within 150 feet or so of the booster target. We were afraid to go closer because the thing was tumbling and gyrating wildly, like a huge, enraged animal. That big moose had gone wild. I've never seen anything that big move so fast. The flashing light had been so erratic and jumpy farther out, in darkness. Now I knew why. Every time that monster rolled over it blanked out the light for several seconds. Then the light would reappear, flash, jump to a new position, jump again, and so on.

We didn't dare go any closer. But that was okay, we didn't have to go closer. We made it and that's what counted.

We were really elated over our success with the rendezvous. So were our friends in Mission Control. The long months of training had paid off, and I had a great sense of fulfillment. A quick check of our reaction control system showed we had used a little more fuel than was planned for this phase of the mission but were in good shape as far as the total mission was concerned.

Most of the extra fuel was used during the closing minutes of rendezvous. Wally hosed out an awful lot in controlling and nulling cross plane velocities (up-down and left-right). It was a tough problem, with the target spinning around like that.

We didn't have much maneuvering propellant—about half as much as later ships had—so we had to be pretty miserly with it. Also, since this was the first flight, we wanted to keep some fuel in reserve for deorbit in case the main rocket engine didn't work. The amount required for deorbit varied according to the weight of the spacecraft and the orbit we were in: the heavier and higher we were, the more it would take to get down. Our red line for fuel quantity decreased throughout the flight as we burned off main rocket fuel and worked our way into lower orbits. We had a "how goes it" chart to help us keep track of fuel consumption as the mission wore on. We had to rely on Mission Control for quantity calculations based on telemetered signals from the spacecraft.

I hadn't slept much the first night. By bedtime the second night, after the rendezvous and all, I was really pooped and had no trouble falling asleep for a solid eight hours.

After the rendezvous most of the flight was pretty much routine and unexciting. But that was as it should be, really—the fewer surprises, the better chance we had of staying up the full eleven days. Not that we were bored, either—there always seemed to be enough to do. We had a little trouble with one of the three fuel cells overheating, but we could solve that by taking it offline for a while and letting it cool down. The water evaporators, used for heat rejection in the environmental control system, dried out and shut off now and then and were a real nuisance to start up, but we didn't really need them. The ship stayed cool enough with only the coolant radiators in operation.

We had a little problem with water accumulating in cold places inside the cabin. It would form in golf-ball-sized globs on coolant pipes. Beneath the center couch we would find a pint or quart of water between the "floor"—really the back side of the main heat shield—and the white glass fiber bag where our pressure suits were stowed. Occasionally, water would form in one of the suit hoses we had rigged to transport cabin air to and from the conditioning unit in the environmental system. We could tell when water was in the hose by the slurping noise. To get rid of the water, we used the overboard dump equipment that normally disposed of urine. We found that we could disconnect the overboard dump line from the urine collection bag and use the open end of the line like a vacuum cleaner to suck up the water.

One of the most surprisingly beautiful moments was the blinding snowstorm of particles that drifted away from the spacecraft when we dumped water or urine overboard. At sunset or sunrise, *Apollo 7* would make a shadow against the cloud, like a dark funnel in the middle of the white snow. One time, the spacecraft was perfectly silhouetted against the cloud, and I could see our outline down to our big engine bell.

The spacecraft made a lot of gurgling, hissing, and thumping sounds. Evidently, main rocket fuel slopped around in the tanks back in the service module every time we rotated the ship or did any thrusting with the small reaction control maneuvering rockets. Those little rockets had a sound all their own, too. The pitch and yaw thrusters, when fired in short bursts—pulse mode, we called it—made resonant, musical thumps. The pitch jets were a higher frequency—about "C" above middle C, I'd say—and the yaw jets were a half-octave or so lower. They didn't really ring—it sounded more like "plink" and "plunk."

With a few more notes we could have played "Yankee Doodle." The roll jets weren't musical at all. They just went "thud." All these peculiar noises gave the impression that we were flying a large tub or barrel half full of water. And I suppose we were, in a way. The service module was a large, mostly empty, and presumably resonant cylinder that did contain fluids of diverse sorts in a variety of tanks and bottles. Come to think of it, before the flight I had wanted to call our ship "Rub-a-Dub-Dub" but no one else thought much of the idea.

We weren't allowed to name our ship anything, as a matter of fact. James Webb, the NASA administrator, didn't like it. He was a real sore head in some ways, and stuffy as hell. He wanted the entire agency to be faceless, amorphous, impersonal—except for himself, of course. He was forceful, dynamic, flamboyant—and his ego could not tolerate the competition of other personalities, like the astronauts. He had a particular dislike for the Mercury guys because once they tried to go over his head to Congress and the president to get an additional Mercury flight approved. The flight would have been Al Shepard's, and at the time there seemed to be good technical reasons for it, but I wonder if the whole thing wasn't merely an effort to get Shepard into orbit (his first flight was only suborbital). In fact, I wonder if Al had made orbit in Mercury whether he would have hung around for an Apollo flight. He must have eaten his heart out all those years, some days crying on his way to the bank(s), feeling cut off, left out, and denied his legacy as an original Mercury astronaut.

Jim Webb's successor, Tom Paine, was a different man altogether. A gentle, sensitive man, he had wit, wisdom, and humor. Our first encounter came right after splashdown: Paine puckishly sent us all navy submariners' dolphin insignia as recognition of our sensational upside-down landing. On the strength of this unplanned test of the uprighting system and a few wrinkles we ironed out in flight, Paine was impelled to announce that *Apollo 7* was a little better than perfect: 101 percent successful.

Despite his fine qualities, the space agency fared poorly under Paine compared to its heyday under Webb. This I attribute more to the tenor of the times than to any superiority of leadership. Webb came in with everything going for him: strong presidential endorsement, good connections in a willing and receptive Congress (his close friend Senator Bob Kerr of Oklahoma got him the job), and the sheer weight and momentum of public acclaim and enthusiasm. I don't know whether he sensed the coming debacle or not, but his timing was perfect. He rode the crest of NASA's popularity wave for seven years, then got off just before it broke. By the time Tom Paine came along, the bloom was off the rose. Nixon came to power with words of praise but no real support for the program. Kerr, Kennedy, and other strong proponents for space in the early sixties were otherwise no longer in power. And the fickle public began clamoring for a new act to follow.

Meanwhile we kept circling the earth once every ninety minutes: a complete day-night cycle every hour and a half. The sunrises and sunsets were incredibly beautiful—and so was the earth as it whirled by beneath us, like a giant diorama in the sky.

We all had minor problems during our flight. Wally was constipated, Walt didn't like the food, and I couldn't sleep—except, perversely, when I wasn't supposed to. Wally and Walt got cabin fever. Walt made it worse with his daily ritual of scratching the date off his wrist calendar. I didn't get "go home fever" until the very last day, which was a very long one for me. The three of us got miserable with head colds that didn't go away until after the flight. With no gravity, our sinuses could not drain. My head felt like it was stuffed and tamped full of cotton like a rag doll. Before the flight somebody asked us why we were taking nine large boxes of tissues. We said we didn't know exactly but they might come in handy. They did. We used up all but one box blowing our noses incessantly for a week. Dispensing of the soiled tissues became a problem at first. Then we hit upon the idea of stuffing them back in the same containers they came out of. To avoid confusion we labeled the ones holding dirty Kleenex. I kept one as a souvenir (but not the tissues)—it says "SNOT."

A bowel movement is something of an event in a spacecraft. The facilities are incredibly primitive, and the odor in so small a space is overpowering. The cabin gas filters remove the smell quickly and it's all over in a minute or two, but that one minute is a beaut. I tried to do mine when the others were asleep. That seemed the most charitable and least embarrassing. Another reason was that the cabin was crowded when all three of us were awake and moving about. The other guys did the same for me. But one time Walt woke me out of a sound sleep—one of those rare occasions when I could sleep—with an aroma so devastating I fancied I'd stuck my head down the smoke stack of a paper mill. Wally found great amusement in my scrambling to get the emergency breathing masks. I fell asleep again with the mask on and the merciful relief it afforded.

Our daily television production, the "Wally, Walt, and Donn Show," got off to a bad start when we refused to do the first scheduled appearance the second day out. The flight plan called for TV shortly before the first main rocket engine burn. We were preoccupied with preparations for that critical exercise and didn't want to divert our attention with what seemed to be trivialities at the time. Our preflight encounters with the TV camera had been less than encouraging. We had seen some pictures that were nothing but blurs, had some difficulty with the power cable, and we felt foreboding of the hassle that was sure to ensue if the thing didn't work. Down at Mission Control the reporters would be bugging the NASA public affairs types who would in turn lean on the flight controllers, and they would be after us to try a variety of their innovative procedures to get a good picture. We thought it would be better to wait until the third day, after our rendezvous was over and when we wouldn't be so busy with firing the engine for the first time and with executing a rendezvous with no radar. Then, if we had a problem, we could take our time and solve it right.

Evidently the earth people felt differently; there was a real stink about the hotheaded, recalcitrant *Apollo 7* crew who wouldn't take orders. Sometime before the flight we had asked our flight planners and the public affairs guys to delete one item from our flight plan, but apparently our request had fallen through a crack.

The next day we did our first TV show and it came off perfectly. I felt a little foolish after the fuss we had made the day before—Wally had been mean as hell about it—and I guess you could say that we erred on the conservative side. But I'd rather we did that than run the risk of jeopardizing our critical test objectives and perhaps the mission itself. In fact, that has been my approach to flying in general. There are a lot of aviators of intrepid derring-do who are no longer with us.

The television episode was typical of our experience during the evolution of Apollo. We were frequently at odds with somebody. It's amazing how many people there were who would unwittingly risk the mission and even our lives. Very early I learnt never to trust anyone's judgment completely out of that entire lash-up of engineers, managers, and technicians. I might also include physicians. *Apollo 1* would seem to be a good example of what happens when you do. We were insolent, high-handed, and Machiavellian at times. Call it paranoia, call it smart—it got the job done. We had a great flight. Anything less might have meant the end of the program. And I'd rather be called a shithead and live through it than have everybody remember what a nice guy I was.

Anyway, the television show was a big hit once we got rolling with it. We weren't too busy after the third day, because most of our tests were crammed into the early part of the flight so we would have most of it if we had to come down early. Consequently we had plenty of the time to devote to TV programming. We heard our ratings were great, but ten days is a very short season.

8. The Grandeur of Earth

I watched the earth roll past the spaceship windows. Earth is a fascinating thing to watch from two hundred miles up. We managed to put on film a great deal of what we saw, but a camera cannot capture the sweeping grandeur and dynamism as whole oceans and continents pass below in minutes. There were thunderstorms at night that looked like frosted light bulbs blinking at random. In daylight they were puffs of cotton. Dunes rippled across a light-tan desert that spread its sands to the base of distant purple mountains. As we sped on, dark-green forests came into view. Great plains of pale yellow and green stretched to the far gray horizon. Rivers snaked across the land like twisted silver ribbons.

I remember once passing over the north coast of Africa and seeing in the distance the entire southern coast of Europe. I got a fantastic view of the North African coastline and all of the Mediterranean Sea. There was Morocco, Algeria, Tunisia, Libya—and the trackless waste of the Sahara Desert to the south. As I looked northward I saw in the distance Sicily, Greece, the Aegean Sea—and there was the island of Cyprus. Then, directly below, the green Nile River valley, the Red Sea, the Sinai Peninsula—an entire continent went by in minutes.

Another time we flew down a chain of islands in the Pacific for two thousand miles. The islands were little rings, ribbons, and blobs of light green or brown embedded in the velvety deep blue of the ocean. A halo of light-green water encircled most of them.

There were some parts of New Guinea and Indonesia that hadn't been seen from orbit before because they were always under clouds. But we were lucky—the clouds parted and I got some good pictures of the New Guinea coastline.

It was almost like a big map except for one thing: you couldn't see any man-made boundary lines between countries. It's funny, all those countries look the same from up there. They're lovely, but you can't tell where one ends and the other begins. I'd never thought about it. You could see natural boundaries, like coastlines and rivers. But those lines they print on maps to separate one country from another—well, they just aren't there.

With a world so rich and beautiful, you would think humans could learn to get along with one another. I guess it's just human nature to fight. Mankind has always had to struggle to get what we need. And after all, we are different from the animals. Maybe that's the trouble. Humans think they are so important. And they are never satisfied. The more they get, the more they think they need.

The world looked so beautiful from that lofty perch—I wondered why we must have wars and poverty and pollution. I realized that the abundant earth will sustain us forever with air to breathe, water to drink, and all the other good things we need—if we take care of it. Mankind needs the earth but the earth does not need mankind. Our survival is all up to us.

There was the Los Angeles basin, all covered with dirty brown smog, blanketing the city. The infamous smog presented itself as a brown smudge with tentacles thrust across the mountains to the east and into the Mojave Desert, spreading like cancer toward the ocean and southward toward San Diego. I could recall occasionally sniffing the obscene stuff years earlier at Edwards Air Force Base, in the desert ninety miles from Los Angeles, oozing its fingers across the mountains onto the clear clean desert beyond.

And now we were passing Arizona, where I learned to fly jets; New Mexico, where I served as a test pilot; and west Texas, where I first soloed an airplane.

As we crossed India, I could see its green plains and forests and the white snowcapped peaks of the Himalayas, the tallest mountains in the world; from there they were just little bumps on the face of our planet—wrinkles in the skin of mother earth. But the mountains were beautiful, their whiteness sparkling in patterned splendor of shadows from peaks and valleys, in brilliant and stark contrast to the soft greenness to the south, as well as the red-brown color of the high Tibetan desert to the north and surrounding lesser mountains below the snow line.

We saw grass fires raging in Australia, and rivers everywhere disgorging their brown vomitus of silt and filth into bays and seas.

It's amazing what we could see of the world from up there: mountain ranges, ocean currents, cloud patterns—entire weather systems swirling around beneath us. We saw and photographed Hurricane Gladys in the Gulf of Mexico—a huge white pinwheel with a little hole right in the center. There was a white button of clouds floating above the hole—a little cap sitting over the eye—and long, thin spiral arms that reached out hundreds of miles.

In contrast to the spidery Gladys, Typhoon Gloria in the Pacific spread a solid mass of gray-white hummocks a thousand miles in all directions from her baleful, malevolent eye in the center. It was enormous. From one horizon to the other all I could see were white clouds. It must have been two thousand miles across. The eye alone, at the center, was over fifty miles wide. That was really some eye! To my mind the cloudy hummocks were welts raised in the earth's hide as Gloria, the frenzied Amazon, lashed and tore at her gentle captive. The spectacle of this awesome monstrosity appeared all the more sinister as I contemplated the wretched souls caught in the storm's fury and the unspeakable horrors they must have endured in the midst of nature's elements gone berserk.

Of all the photos I took on the flight, I prize most the one I took of Gloria's eye. Wally and Walt were asleep and I had the ship to myself. These were the quiet hours of the flight, and in order to save electric power and rocket fuel we had shut down all our attitude control systems. Thus the spacecraft was free to roll and toss about at random as we coasted along our orbital path through space. There were five viewing windows: two on the sides, two looking forward, and one in the hatch that gave a view roughly perpendicular to the line of sight through the forward windows. The windows were quite small, only a few inches across, but I could get a decent field of view by pressing my face close against the glass. The hatch window was the largest, a circle of glass about twelve inches across, but the worst for viewing because water had condensed between the panes and formed droplets and rivulets on the glass. I could see through it by moving my head to look through the small clear spaces between the blobs of water, but the hatch window was useless for photography.

Because of the ship's motion I had to move rapidly from one window to another to keep the earth in view. And at times the earth would disappear altogether for a minute or two. Trying to anticipate which window would next give the best view turned out to be an amusing mental exercise in spatial relations. There was never any particular pattern or sequence that I could count on to repeat itself. It all depended on the ship's motion and the direction it happened to be pointing in space. I had developed considerable skill in moving my body quickly about the spacecraft. I used my feet to grasp one of the struts that held our couches in place, and with that single point of leverage I was able to arc myself from one side to the other, stopping precisely to face any window I chose. My two feet served as a restraint or anchor to prevent my drifting about and left both hands free to operate the cameras.

"*Apollo 7*, this is Houston. How do you read, over?"

Across the miles, halfway around the earth, came the voice of our capcom, Ron Evans.

"Roger, Houston, Seven, read you loud and clear. Donn, the flight director wishes to advise that on your next pass across the Pacific you'll go over Typhoon Gloria."

"Okay, Ron. I think we went over part of it on this rev. Is that what all those clouds were?"

"Yeah, probably. There's a good chance you'll pass over the eye next time. Be on the lookout for it."

"Roger, I'll give an eye for an eye."

A slight pause, then Ron came back. "That's not bad for an amateur, but Gerry says you ought to get a new writer."

"Well, we save all the good ones for the TV show."

"You call that stuff good?"

"It's the best we can do on location. And you have to admit, we've got a hell of a location!"

"Right you are."

"Hey, Ron, can you give me a time hack for the eye of that storm? I just might get lucky and get a picture if I know when to look."

"Roger, we'll get you a time hack. Stand by one."

Ron Evans conferred with the flight controllers manning the consoles in Mission Control. A minute later he came back on the net. "*Apollo 7*, Houston, your approximate time of passage for the eye of Gloria is one oh one hours one zero minutes GET. That's one oh one plus one oh. Over."

"Roger, oh one plus ten. Can you give me some idea of where it will be north or south of track?"

There was another short conference, followed by: "*Apollo 7*, we can't give you that. Also, that time hack is only approximate. It could be a minute or two either way."

"Hey, you don't have our position any better than that?"

"No sweat. We've got your orbit cold, but we don't know where the storm is. We have it on a weather satellite photo, but it's twelve hours old. The storm may have moved quite a bit since then. If you get a visual on it, try to get a good time hack as well as a picture. The weather people would like to know."

"Okay, Ron, I'll do my best."

It would be difficult to get an accurate position and a photograph at the same time. I glanced at our mission clock: 100 hours and 31 minutes since liftoff. Almost 40 minutes until we're over the storm. Plenty of time to get ready. And only 160 hours until splashdown—160 hours! That's almost a week!

There were little crevices above the hatch where the top of the main display console attached to the wall. We had discovered the little crack was a good place to stow checklists, flight plans, and the like. I reached up and withdrew the orbit map that we used to plot our position over the earth along our flight path. It wasn't too accurate, but it was good enough to plan ahead an orbit or two for photographs and earth observations. As I plotted our position at one oh one plus ten, I noticed that one of our tracking ships, the USNS *Mercury,* was shown to be in the same general area. If the map was correct, they were getting clobbered by Typhoon Gloria.

"Houston, *Apollo 7.* Is the tracking ship *Mercury* still on station? According to my map they're catching hell from that storm."

"Affirmative. The *Mercury* is still on station. They report hurricane winds and violent sea state. They are going to stay put and ride it out."

"I see. Very good. Give them our regards and tell 'em to hang in there."

I had visions of the ship heaving, pitching, lunging into mountainous waves, the crew being tossed against bulkheads, their footing made all the more treacherous by the slime of vomit on the deck.

"Seven, we just got another report: The crew of the *Mercury* wish to announce that they are green, but not with envy."

My laughter woke Walt. He chuckled gently at my recounting of the *Mercury* episode, and Wally grumbled sleepily something about holding down the noise and what the hell is Walt doing awake anyway, he is supposed to be sleeping. Then they both rolled over and went back to sleep.

"Houston, Seven, Roger the *Mercury* status report. I laughed so hard it woke Walt and Wally. I think we had better hold down the chatter."

"Roger, Seven. We're coming up to LOS [loss of signal] in one minute, anyway. I've got a flight plan update for you and some block data but we'll wait until AOS [acquisition of signal] Hawaii. We would also like a report on Typhoon Gloria at that time."

"Roger, Houston, Seven out."

The mission clock now read 100 hours, 36 minutes. I set the event timer to count down from 34 minutes, the time remaining to our passage of Typhoon Gloria. At that moment a crackling, hissing sound in my headset told me our S-band receiver had broken lock and we were no longer in contact with Mission Control. I turned down my S-band volume and made a mental note to turn it up again in forty minutes in anticipation of Hawaii AOS. To time this interval I started one of my two wrist stopwatches. I carried two because I had gotten into the habit of relying on them in training. The event timers in our simulator never worked well. The use of stopwatches turned out to be a good procedure, because one of our two event timers in the spacecraft ceased to function about halfway through the flight.

We were in darkness now, and I noticed that according to the flight plan sunrise would occur about seven or eight minutes before the estimated time of arrival at the center of the typhoon. The first two or three minutes of daylight are nearly useless for a visual search, and if the ETA were two minutes off I might have only two or three minutes to search for the storm, locate the eye, and get a picture. If the ship happened to be pointing the wrong way, I might miss it altogether.

There might also be a problem in determining camera settings. Our photo experts had given us standard settings for various lighting conditions and earth features, but Wally had eschewed the settings in favor of the exposure meter we carried. I decided to use the standard settings and modify them with a meter reading if I could get one. I set the camera, mounted it and the exposure meter on the wall next to the hatch, then let myself go limp in the relaxed levitation of weightlessness to await the arrival of daylight.

As it always did, sunrise burst upon the earth's curved horizon in a brilliant flash of color—thin bright bands of intense red, green, and blue. It only lasted a few seconds, but that one view of sunrise in space is worth all the years of preparation for the flight. I noted with satisfaction that the ship appeared to be moving in a manner that would keep our part of the earth in view most of the time. My feet seized a couch strut and I twisted myself around to pull the camera and exposure meter off the wall. Sunlight flooded the earth, and I began scanning for the storm through the windows.

I saw only the ocean at first, very dark blue, with occasional patches of dark-gray clouds. No sign of the typhoon. To get a wide view I had to look through all the windows in rapid sequence. At any instant one would be looking straight down while one or two others would give oblique views, perhaps out to the horizon. Another window usually looked out upon the blackness of empty space. The whole effect was one of being inside a bug's eye, each facet giving only a segment of the total view.

The clouds thickened and turned a lighter shade of gray. As we sped eastward toward higher sun angles, some of the cloud masses took on a pinkish hue. As the spacecraft rolled, the hatch window turned to offer a slanting view forward to the horizon along our track. There ahead of us I could see for the first time what I had been searching for: a solid mass of lumpy clouds reaching to the horizon and as far as I could see to the left and right. Typhoon Gloria!

In contrast to the hurricane, there was no particular pattern or swirling appearance. The low sun angle heightened the relief of the hummocks and depressions. Here and there, little pimples of boiling clouds erupted through the upper surface, like pus oozing from open wounds.

I scrutinized all the dimples and depressions in the clouds that came into view, but none looked like the center of a storm. The spacecraft continued its lazy rolling and tumbling, and sometimes the storm would disappear for several seconds. It was possible that during one of these brief intervals the eye could slip by without my seeing it. Then at length a large depression appeared near the horizon, merely a dark line at first, but deeper and longer than the others I had seen. It was coming directly at us, and as it drew closer it took the form of a round hole in the clouds. I could see the steep wall of clouds that rimmed its perimeter and a spot of cloud in the center of the black hole. It had form, it had depth, and it even had a pupil—an eyeball indeed! This gigantic sinister orb glaring up at me seemed to embody the total and consummate evils of all time. The wicked living thing had an ominous quality that sent a shiver of fear and revulsion through me.

As we went across the center of the storm, the ship rolled so that one window pointed straight down. I was so fascinated by the awesome specter below that I almost forgot to take a photograph. But I had the camera ready and click—there! Got it! I managed to catch one shot with the Hasselblad as the right-side window turned to look straight down at the evil eye. But I had to be quick—a few seconds later the spacecraft rolled again, and the storm was gone from view. I noted the time on the mission clock and wrote it on the flight plan. We were fifty seconds early. Not bad, except that fifty seconds is worth 250 miles at orbital speed.

9. Return to Earth

Six hours until entry, and Walt and Wally were asleep. I was supposed to wake them soon but I wanted to get the platform aligned first. Might as well let them sleep, I decided. There wasn't much for them to do until I finished the alignment. I was a whole revolution ahead of the flight plan. We were fat on fuel cell reactants for electric power and I decided to power up the guidance system and align the platform early. We were a little skimpy on reaction control thruster fuel, but I had learned to align the platform without benefit of stabilizing the spacecraft attitude. There was plenty of reaction fuel for normal pre-entry maneuvers, but we wanted to save all we could in case we had to use our attitude control thrusters for the deorbit burn. That is, in the unlikely event that the main rocket engine would crap out. There wasn't much chance of that. We had had seven consecutive good firings and . . .

"*Apollo 7*, this is Houston, over."

Oh Christ, Houston, shut up, I thought. I had both hands on the optics controls and wasn't about to let go to squeeze the mike button. It had taken me ten minutes to pull my first alignment star, Antares, into the center of the telescope. With the ship in a random tumble, I wasn't about to blow it and start over merely to talk to Houston. The computer was flashing VERB 51. In machine parlance that meant "Mark a star." Antares drifted to the center of the crosshairs. I pushed the Mark button and caught it, spot on.

"*Apollo 7*, Houston, how do you read, over?"

"Houston, Seven, stand by. I'm aligning the IMU."

"Roger, we're reading your computer on the downlink, but we're starting to lose data. Request you switch to Omni antenna D. That's Omni Delta."

Oh crap. Big brothers are watching but can't see it all. Pretty soon they will want to be up here in the cockpit with us. I floated backward, ducked my head to clear the bottom of the main display panel, reached across, and flipped the antenna switch to D.

"Roger, Houston, Omni D. You have it."

"Thanks, Donn. We've got a good lock on now. When you're ready, we have some entry data for you."

"Okay, give me a couple of minutes."

"Take your time. We have a twelve-minute station pass."

A gentle pull on a couch strut sent me drifting slowly back to the optics panel. The star pattern in the telescope told me we had drifted several degrees. The initial alignment would be off quite a bit, but there were two good stars, Antares and Nunki, in the field of view. I could recycle the computer and repeat the procedure in a matter of seconds.

The second time through, the computer displayed four zeroes and a five for the star difference angle: an alignment error of five hundredths of a degree.

"We read four balls five. You're getting sloppy."

"You guys sure are nosy. I'll do better next time."

I floated over to the right couch and withdrew the PAD (preliminary advisory data) book from a box. A flashlight started to drift out, but I closed the lid before it could get loose. A nuisance now, a floating dense object could become a menace during entry and landing. I turned to the section of the book labeled "Entry."

"Houston, go ahead with your data. I'm ready to copy."

"Roger. And can we have the computer? Guido can load the numbers for you while I call them up to you."

"Splendid. Go ahead, guido. You've got the computer."

Through the S-band link, the guidance officer could control the computer and load numbers directly into its memory. The ritual of writing down the numbers and reading them back to Mission Control, to be certain we got them right, was a backup procedure. We used this PAD data to verify and cross-check the numbers loaded in by guido through the command link over S-band. The procedure was a good one, especially for critical events like entry, because once in a while the data from guido didn't load properly and we would have to punch them in by hand from our PAD data. The computer itself functioned without a flaw, but we gummed up the works a few times by loading in bad numbers and making procedural errors in operating it. By starting the guidance and control operations early, we always had time to rectify the problems if the machine went awry.

". . . plus two two eight, oh seven. Nine three. Minus one six five oh two . . . *Apollo 7*, read back."

"Houston, I guess you could say I've got your number!"

A period of silence followed. Then, "Oh brother, you get worse all the time."

"Sorry about that. After ten days in this can I'm getting punn-chy."

I imagined the controllers back in Houston groaning softly to themselves. Capcom offered no comment, reluctant to evoke another corny response.

Shortly thereafter, Wally and Walt wakened. Walt stuck his head up from below the couch, bleary-eyed and confused. The fullness in his face from being weightless accented the creases and lines that made him look old. His ten-day stubble of beard deepened the haggard appearance brought on by the week-old nagging head cold that had afflicted all of us. He flashed a foolish grin and asked, "Are we really going home?"

"Yeah, man, today's the day," I replied. "Five hours to retro. The IMU is up and aligned, the computer is loaded and ready to go. Let's get some breakfast. We have a lot to do yet."

Wally grumped and groaned as he emerged from his cocoon-like sleep restraint beneath the left couch. "What the hell was all that chatter about? It sounded like you and capcom were having a regular tea party," he rasped with a sullen scowl. Often he was grouchy on waking, and a flap the prior night with Mission Control over not wearing our helmets for entry hadn't helped any.

"Nothing in particular. Mostly the PAD update," I monotoned.

"Well, you sure made a racket." He paused and added, "Oh, what the hell is the difference? We're going home now anyway." His expression turned to intense concern. "We *are* 'go' for retro, aren't we?"

I assured him that we were, and gave a brief status report on the spacecraft.

We prepared our meal—the last one of the flight—and ate it. Eating in a spacecraft is rather unusual. Our food was freeze-dried; we added water to it in plastic bags and mixed it up to eat it. We also had some bite-size cubes of concentrated food—candy, cookies, and bacon squares. Some of it was pretty good and I guess we could get along on it for a few days—but it was not exactly like home cooking. The food would get better on later flights, but we were stuck with what we had.

I would reach in the food drawer and withdraw a fist-sized foil package. A small white label stuck on it said the day and meal number, such as "Day 1, Meal 3." I would peel back the foil and take out some shriveled-looking plastic bags about a foot long. To give a meal example, one bag contained a small quantity of pale green powder and was labeled "Pea Soup." Another, containing cocoa-colored powder, was marked "Chocolate Pudding." Wrapped in a third bag was a small, hard, pinkish brick that looked a lot like dry, stale bread. This bag was labeled "Spaghetti w/ Meat Sauce." A patch of purplish powder marked "Grape Drink" completed the assortment. None of it looked at all appetizing.

A pistol-shaped water gun hung loosely on the wall near the optics panel. I took the gun and inserted the nozzle into the grape drink bag. Each time I squeezed the trigger, a small charge of water shot into the bag. I squeezed the bag a few times and the water turned murky, then bright purple as the powder dissolved. I unrolled the soft plastic mouthpiece and took a few swallows. Mmm, pretty good.

Hot water for the spaghetti came from a small tube in a panel near the equipment bay. I pushed the spaghetti bag into the hot water tube and pressed the plunger button next to it several times. Hot water squirted into the bag in small spurts. I sloshed the bag gently and stuck it on the wall. Velcro held the bag in place. As I watched, the hard pink brick softened and turned into short lengths of white spaghetti, bits of brown meat, and bright red tomato sauce. Imagine, spaghetti with sauce from water and a dried-up little cake. Was it any good? I don't think it would go over too well at the Bakersfield Gourmet Club, but it wasn't too bad.

I'd stuff the food bags into my suit pockets. With my knees I would push myself off the wall and float lazily into the center crew couch. I'd snap the lap belt loosely across my hips and unroll the mouthpiece on the pea soup, which I had prepared along with the chocolate pudding while the spaghetti was soaking. I'd put the mouthpiece in my mouth, squeeze the bottom end of the bag and gulp to swallow as the thick green ooze filled my throat. Not bad, if you don't mind eating through a hose.

What is the Bakersfield Gourmet Club? It's a long story.

As you might guess from the name, the Bakersfield Gourmet Club is a group of people in Bakersfield, California, who like to eat good food. They formed this club and met once a month at a certain restaurant for a specially prepared delicacy. I had to go there once, to speak after dinner. Did I have a nice time? Not really. The club president was pleasant enough. And the people there were curious to meet an astronaut. I think a lot of folks think we're freaks. But no one there gave a rap about space or about what I had to say. With their bellies stuffed, a lot of them went to sleep right after dessert.

Why did they invite me? I was a drawing card, an attraction to perk up attendance. The president told me that attendance at the dinners had been poor, and the club was losing money. So he called on the local newspaper editor, who leaned on the congressman from Bakersfield, who in turn pressured the space agency into sending an astronaut to the Bakersfield Gourmet Club. I guess it worked. Practically all the members showed up.

How did they happen to pick me? It was my week in the barrel, as we called it. Every so often—usually about once a year—each astronaut had to drop what he was doing and travel about the country all week making speeches and appearances that were set up by some guys at NASA headquarters in Washington. Most of the time we were not supposed to appear publicly unless it was something really special, like a big conference or a national meeting of some kind. But when it was your week in the barrel anything could happen—like the Gourmet Club.

I wouldn't have minded so much if I had been in California, anyway. We spent a lot of time, as you know, working on the spacecraft out there while they were building it in Downey. But as it was, I had the rest of the week on the East Coast. I had to make two cross-country flights in two days, just to talk to forty people who would rather eat and sleep.

Some astronauts liked making speeches, and some didn't. I didn't mind once in a while, if the event was worthwhile and people were interested in hearing what I had to say. The space program is expensive, and I figured the taxpayers had a right to know what the money is being spent for.

You got to meet a lot of people, traveling around like that. But you didn't get to know anyone very well. It was dash in, dash out, and on to the next engagement. If we hadn't flown our own planes we could never have made the schedule they laid out for us.

The spaghetti with meat sauce wasn't bad, either. Life up there in space was pretty nice.

When we had finished eating, I pulled the release on the buckle of my lap belt. It was time to clean up the cabin. I stuffed the food bags down the trash locker. We didn't want all those little crumbs floating around. On Earth, you find those crumbs under the table when people eat. Up there, those little bits of food could cause a lot of trouble. They could float around and get in the air conditioning system and gum up the works. The air in the cabin, which is really mostly oxygen, circulated through filters that absorbed odors and took out the excess carbon dioxide that we made when we breathed. And the cabin air was heated or cooled so it stayed at the right temperature.

Of course, we couldn't just open the door once in a while and get some fresh air. What's out there? Nothing, that's what. There's no air to breathe, nothing but a vacuum in outer space. If we'd opened that hatch all the air in there would have rushed out in a great whoosh, and we would all have died in seconds. There was no air to breathe anywhere except right there in that capsule and down there on the earth. Suddenly the earth seemed quite small.

What would have happened if we'd sprung a leak? If any little bit leaks out or is used up, more oxygen comes in from some storage tanks back in the service module. And for big leaks, well, we didn't expect to have any. But if we did, we would have hurried and put on our space suits again.

There was a lot of food left over that none of us wanted. Puddings, hot chocolate, cookies: all rich, sweet, concentrated stuff. A few of the meat dishes were still palatable, but the only thing that really still tasted good was bacon squares. We had eaten them all except for a few that I had ratholed earlier in the flight. I put a couple of squares away as souvenirs and shared the rest with Walt and Wally. The day before entry, Walt offered to swap his entire day's rations for two bacon squares. I thought back to our preflight preparations.

"Did you guys get a chance to look over your menus yet?" asked Malcolm Smith, our doctor in charge of space food. Smith, a trim youthful man with soft gray eyes and wavy hair, had a droll sense of humor, an engaging manner, and a boyish smile that belied his maturity and dedication.

Walt looked up from his habitual fingernail scraping and grinned at Malcolm. "Yeah, we did. Donn and I think you're too heavy on the bite-size. How come so much?"

"Well, the bite-size has a very high nutritional content," said Smith earnestly.

"You mean higher than the rehydratables? I don't understand that," I remarked skeptically.

"Well, not exactly," continued Malcolm. "What I mean is we can get more calories per pound, and pack it in less volume, with the bite-size foods." He paused, smiled, and added, "You know, we have a weight limit for the food, like everything else on the stowage list."

"Yeah, I know, Malcolm, but that bite-size stuff is heavy, rich, concentrated. You eat that stuff for a day or two and you're fed up. We know that from the Gemini flights," said Walt sharply. "And you know it, too," he added, waggling his finger at Smith for emphasis.

"That's right, Walt," replied Malcolm with a sigh. "But I'd like you to try this menu for four days and see how it goes. If you don't like it, we can change it."

"Now, just a minute," barked Walt with indignation. "I've already sampled every item on your list of food items and rated them on the preference sheets, like you asked us. This menu doesn't reflect my choices in the slightest. What was the point of going through that rain dance if you weren't going to pay any attention to the ratings? There's no sense in running a four-day food test when I already know it's unacceptable."

Smith frowned and pursed his lips. He shrugged and said, "Walt, I did try to use your preferred items. But you can't eat the same food every day; you'd get tired of it. Then there's the weight problem, and nutritional balance, and . . ."

"Hold it, guys," I interrupted. "Malcolm, I know you've done the best you can with all the constraints you have to work with. But Walt's right. There's no point in trying to force ourselves onto a diet that we're not going to like. Let's face it, even our best choices aren't exactly gourmet delights. Why don't you do this: go back and make up menus based on our selections, and don't worry about the weight. We'll try it out for four days. If it's okay, but too heavy, we'll negotiate a weight increase with the project office. If they can't give a few pounds for food, this whole program is out of whack."

"All right, I'll do that. I'd rather give you Pillsbury's best than Smith's worst," said Malcolm, smiling.

At that moment, Wally popped through the door. "Is that anything like knockwurst? I'll have two, with a side dish of sauerkraut," he said with a smug grin.

I knew I'd been had; Wally had one-upped me again on puns. "No fair!" I cried. "We didn't see you coming!"

Malcolm Smith chuckled softly. Walt put his hand to his face and groaned.

"How are we doing with our entry checklist? Are we on the timeline?" Wally's question brought my wandering mind back abruptly to the immediate circumstance.

"Right. In fact, we're a little ahead. I've stowed most of the loose gear except what we need for deorbit. The guidance system is powered up and the IMU is all aligned. I've done a nav check to verify the state vector, I've checked the target load for the burn, and we have a maneuver PAD and a preliminary update. I also got some of the systems checks out of the way before you guys woke up."

"What's left?" asked Walt.

"It's all in the flight plan," I answered. "Change canisters, check the entry monitor system, get the secondary evaporator on—if you can—align the platform and . . ."

"I thought you had already done that," uttered Wally in a hoarse, thick voice.

"What?"

"Aligned the platform—the IMU!" he crackled with some irritation.

"I did, but we have to realign using option three to set it up for entry," I replied.

"I don't see why we have to do everything twice," Wally snorted.

Aw, shit, I thought. We went over all that three months ago with the flight controllers.

"We also have to get our lumpy suits on. That is, unless you want to piss off the world and enter in shirtsleeves," I volunteered, changing the subject.

"Oh, Christ, no," interjected Walt. "After all that to-do about the helmets yesterday, they'd have our heads. Besides, the suits provide the only foot restraints we've got. I don't want to bust my shins on the control panel if we have a hard landing."

"Goddammit, I made that decision yesterday," snapped Wally. "We wear the suits without the helmets. The subject is closed for discussion." Captain Bligh had spoken.

With all the talk about head colds, eardrums, and helmets, we had tried to think of some way we could protect our heads without wearing helmets. The headrests on the couches were made to fit the large bubble helmets and therefore were much too big to be of any use in protecting bareheaded crewmen.

"Tape?" Walt replied, when I brought up one idea.

"Yes. You know, the roll of gray tape we have been using to tie up used food bags and waste containers," I said.

"I don't think that would work too well, either," Walt remarked. "I don't see how you could get the tape tight enough to do any good."

We eventually settled on a way to save our skulls and our ears, too. You recall those plastic food bags we tied up with tape? If we took two or three bags, rolled them up together and taped them, they would make a lump about the size of an orange. Then we could tape the balls of plastic to the headrests. They would make perfect bumpers for our heads.

Walt spoke first. "Terrific," he whooped. "I say we try it. What have we got to lose?"

"I'll get the stuff," I said as he leaped into the equipment bay and reached for the roll of tape and some empty food bags inside a storage compartment on the forward bulkhead. I rolled three food bags into a ball and peeled off two strips of the narrow gray tape, which I wrapped crossways around the plastic. I made another roll the same way and taped the two fist-sized lumps to the sides of my headrest, on the inside where my head would lie during entry and landing. I flattened myself out a few inches above the couch, face up. Grabbing the ends of the lap belt for leverage, I pulled myself down onto the couch and forced my head down between the taped plastic bumpers.

"Perfect!" I asserted.

"How does it feel?" asked Walt as he floated in close to inspect the make-shift head restraint.

"Just fine," I said, "as snug and secure as anything you could ask for."

Within minutes Walt and Wally had constructed the same sort of head bumpers for themselves. Each of us carefully fitted and adjusted our "bumpers" to match the exact width and contours of our own head. As a final test of our newly created head restraints, all three of us strapped ourselves to the couches, like three statues laid out stiff and straight, with our heads jammed between those potato-looking lumps. Our impromptu invention fit perfectly, and I felt smug over our cleverness. They reminded me of mouse ears.

Walt chortled to himself softly, but Wally saw nothing funny at all in the observation and furrowed his brow in a sullen frown. I laughed a great guffaw and burst into a loud chorus of the Mickey Mouse Club theme song.

"Oh, for Pete's sake, knock it off!" grumped Wally.

"It's a good thing we are going down soon," Walt grinned at me. "Another day up here and you would be ready for the looney bin."

"Look who's talking," I replied. "Here we are, hundreds of miles up in space, and you wanted to put up the window shades so no one would see in when you went to the bathroom."

"I guess we are all a little nuts," smiled Wally, regaining his good humor.

The next item on our entry prep agenda was donning the suits. They were stuffed into a large L-shaped glass fiber bag beneath my couch. I went down there and pulled out Wally and Walt's suits. There wasn't room for all three of us to put on those stiff, bulky lumpy garments at the same time. The plan was for Walt and Wally to get theirs on while I found some way to cinch down our helmets for entry. We couldn't leave the helmets beneath the couches for entry because they would not allow room for the couch struts to stroke in event of a hard landing. And if the struts didn't stroke, our bodies would have to absorb the energy of impact instead of the crushable honeycomb material inside the struts. As a buck fighter pilot would say, we would bust our asses.

Walt got his suit on in a matter of seconds. He was lithe, agile, and wiry. Wally was thickset and stiff, like a ponderous old bear. We had to get him into the lower equipment bay, where there was more room, and stuff him into the suit. He managed to squirm back into his couch and I had room, finally, to work on the helmet stowage and put on my own suit. I managed to attach the glass-fiber helmet bags, with their little tie-down tabs and snaps, to the floor beneath the leg rests on the couches. Secured to the bottom edge of the front wall in the lower equipment bay, the helmets were still within the couch stroking envelope. But it would take one hell of a jolt on landing to jam the couches against them. And I figured that if that happened it would be a bad day all around.

"How are you coming with the helmets, Donn?" Wally queried.

"Fine, Wally, I'm just about through. I have to tighten the retaining straps on this last one," I replied.

"Better shake a leg. You have to get your suit on and get strapped in yet," he admonished.

"Right. And I have to do the final alignment and attitude star check before I get into the couch," I added.

My own garment popped loose from the stowage bag after a moment's tugging. I let it unfold in the lower equipment bay at the foot of the crew couches and wriggled into my formal astronauts' habit. Wally zipped me up in the back and Walt gave me a hand with the suit hoses, the conduits that carried oxygen between the pressure suit and the environmental control system. The hoses were flexible but springy, and sometimes perversely resisted being connected to the suit.

The alignment was easy. We made side bets with Mission Control on the accuracy of my measurements and won. The computer flashed a star difference reading of zero—"five balls," we called it. The measurement error had to be less than five thousandths of a degree. That was considerably better than the five hundredths, or four balls five, I had gotten earlier. I felt vindicated.

The star data check for proper spacecraft attitude was a different matter. The theory was that if you cranked in the correct shaft and trunnion angles on the optics, and the ship was holding the right orientation in space, you should see a particular star in the sextant. You could move the optics directly by manual controls or through a special routine in the computer. I tried it both ways and got identical results: sunlight instead of the designated star. Obviously, we were pointing in the wrong direction. I consulted our star chart, a celestial map printed on both sides of an eight-inch disc, one of several oracles that made up our on board data kit. If my reckoning was correct, and we fired our rocket engine for deorbit at the appointed time, we would instead soar out into some other, higher orbit from which a safe return would be unlikely.

The big question I had to resolve was the source of the error. Was the inertial platform aligned improperly? Had we gotten bad data from Mission Control? Or had we simply flown to the wrong angles on our attitude instrument? I checked our attitude readout on the computer. It tallied with the indications on the attitude ball: both wrong. Evidently we were simply holding the wrong attitude angles. To put it bluntly, Wally, who had insisted on doing virtually all the manual maneuvering himself, blew it.

"Hey, Wally, uh—I think we've drifted off our attitude a little. The star check didn't work out too well," I declared casually.

"Oh yeah? Hmmm. That's funny. Our attitude seems to be right on, according to the eight ball. Better run your star check again," answered Wally flatly.

Oh boy, I thought. He's pointed wrong and doesn't know it, or doesn't want to admit it.

In the interest of uniformity, we had worked out an arrangement with our flight controllers that all our main engine firings would be done at the same attitude angles with respect to the IMU. Thus each burn had required a special platform alignment, tailored precisely to give the same attitude on the instruments. The only exception was the deorbit burn, which for some peculiar technical reasons required a different platform alignment and consequently a different attitude indication on the attitude ball. Wally had flown to the correct attitude for all previous seven burns—and therefore the wrong direction in space for this one.

"I've already checked it twice, Wally. Read your gimbal angles again. We should be at zero, zero, zero. I'm getting one eighty, one eighty, zero on the DSKY." The DSKY, or "disky," was the computer display and keyboard, the gadget through which we communicated with the onboard computer.

Wally said nothing but gave his hand controller a few deft flicks that set the ship moving toward the correct attitude. Our big tub of a spacecraft rotated ponderously, almost imperceptibly as the numbers on the "disky," representing the gimbal angles, began counting up. When we reached the new orientation, Wally stopped the ship and nulled out the residual rates of motion to near zero. I did the star check again. We were right on for the deorbit burn.

I checked the temperature on the Command Module reaction rockets and found they were high enough that we did not have to do the preheating procedure. We felt relieved at not having to go through that awkward, unwieldy, and time-consuming sequence for several reasons. It required twenty to thirty minutes of precious time during our critical reentry prep period and would delay strapping in my crew couch by that much, since I had to be in the lower equipment bay to operate the heater switch. The heaters themselves consisted of the electric coils used to operate the rocket propellant valves during entry. If we didn't do it right, or even if we did and one of the valves hung open, we could hose out all the fuel or oxidizer and perhaps go out of control when the system was activated for entry. The Command Module RCS heater system was a kluged-up, half-baked "jury rig" that we had fought vociferously to get changed during the design phase of the program, to no avail. It was an exception to the usual norm of design excellence throughout the spacecraft and represented a fine example of the Peter Principle and Parkinson's Law applied to mechanical and electrical design. The reaction control heater system was an illogical, ill-conceived, and potentially dangerous appendage added hastily after the basic RCS system had already been laid out. Further, the need for heaters was questionable since no one had ever proved that the reaction control rockets would not work if they became a little cool.

I got myself ensconced in the center couch with a little difficulty and a lot of help from Walt and Wally. They held the straps for me while I got situated. I cinched up the straps as tightly as I could and jammed my head down between the makeshift head restraints we had constructed to hold our heads still during entry and cushion the impact, if any, on landing.

The last hours of *Apollo 7*'s flight in space passed quickly for us as we prepared for return to Earth. A full hour before entering the upper fringes of the atmosphere, the work was complete. I had aligned the inertial unit, Walt had put away all the loose equipment, and Wally had lined up the ship for the retro burn. All three of us had put on our space suits, except for the clear, bowl-shaped helmets.

After a final inspection of the cabin, we strapped ourselves to the couches. A quick run-through of the entry program reassured us that all the entry data was correct and in order. It matched identically the numbers we had gotten from Mission Control and had written on our entry pad.

I stepped the computer through its thrusting programs in a final rehearsal of our deorbit burn. I pushed the large, numbered square buttons on the computer keyboard.

"What are you doing?" asked Walt.

"Just checking the entry programs," I replied. "Hand me that data book, will you? I want to be sure the right numbers are loaded in the computer."

"I thought we already checked the data load," said Wally.

"We did," I answered. "But I just want to check it again. Besides, we've got another thirty minutes 'til retro burn, and there is nothing else to do."

"Well, don't wear it out," said Wally, pointing to the face of the computer. "We're not down yet, and this thing still has to fly home."

"Don't worry," I said. "The ol' computer won't wear out now. It will get us home, all right."

It sequenced properly and all the numbers looked good. Just then capcom called, interrupting the conversation in the cabin. "*Apollo 7*, Houston here. We have a new weather forecast for your recovery area."

"Fine," Wally called into his microphone. "Go ahead."

"Forecast calls for thin overcast, visibility five miles with light mist. Wave height, three feet."

"That sounds pretty good," Wally transmitted. "What's the weather right now?"

"The latest report we have says the weather presently is scattered clouds and ten-mile visibility. There is a front moving in, but it isn't supposed to reach the area until after you splash down."

"Roger. Thanks, Houston," said Wally.

The recovery area was the place in the ocean where we were supposed to land. There was a ship there, an aircraft carrier called the *Essex*, waiting to pick us up from the ocean as soon as we splashed down. The *Essex* was located in the Atlantic Ocean, near Bermuda. The computer knew the location, since that was part of the data we loaded in a while ago. If the computer and the guidance system did their job, and the *Essex* was where it was supposed to be, we ought to land right on target. But not right on the ship—the spacecraft wasn't built to land on a hard surface.

Wally set up the Entry Monitor System, a device used to cross-check the computer's automatic steering of the spacecraft during entry. The EMS could also give us a backup means to effect a safe entry and a reasonably accurate splashdown under manual control. The EMS acted oddly, and we decided not to count on it either to monitor the progress of entry or to provide ranging data for a manual entry. We would, however, let it run to allow postflight analysis of its malfunction. The EMS was not critical for our flight but could be crucial on later flights coming back from the moon. Walt ran through his systems checks and found the spacecraft to be all in order. One fuel cell was offline due to overheating but would be brought on to give added electric power for the main rocket engine gimbals just before the deorbit burn. After that there was nothing to do but sit back.

After eleven days, we were ready to return to Earth with only the cone-shaped Command Module remaining out of the entire stack of booster rocket and spacecraft. We had stowed all of our loose gear, put on our lumpy space suits, strapped ourselves in, got the IMU aligned, called up the computer's reentry program, and set up the main rocket engine for the deorbit burn. It had worked perfectly seven times. Once more and we were home free. Of course, if it didn't work we still had enough fuel left in our reaction rockets to get us out of orbit—and if they didn't work we could use the control rockets on the Command Module. And in a pinch we could get along without the computer. But we hoped it would all go normally—we needed the data, and besides, we were tired and we wanted to land as close as possible to our recovery ship, the aircraft carrier *Essex*. At this point we had no desire to practice ocean survival for several hours while the recovery force came looking for us.

At five minutes to ignition, Walt began reading the checklist for the eighth and final burn of *Apollo 7*'s powerful rocket. Wally and I threw switches, set controls, and checked meters as Walt called out each step. A few minutes before retro burn we checked the rocket gimbal motors and cycled the computer into the last steps of its thrusting program. The computer began ticking off the seconds to retro fire as we went through the last four steps of our checklist. We gave the computer automatic control of the ship's attitude and the rocket engine.

Down at Mission Control, the retro officer prepared himself for the final countdown. His job was to make sure the calculations were right, and to take charge of the control room operation during this last firing of the rocket that would set *Apollo 7* on course for returning to Earth. Because split-second timing was necessary, to avoid any last minute mix ups the retro officer, rather than capcom, would talk directly to the orbiting astronauts.

"*Apollo 7*, retro here. Are you all set?"

"Hey, retro, nice to hear from you!" Wally called cheerfully. "Roger, we're ready."

"Seven, we're coming up on T minus one minute," said the retro officer. "I'll give you a time hack. Stand by . . . ready . . . Mark! . . . one minute."

"Roger, right on," called Wally as he noted with pleasure that the spacecraft timers were exactly in accord with retro's count.

"Thirty seconds," retro continued at exactly one-half minute before ignition. And then, in a great booming voice, as if he were announcing the coming of the end of the world, he counted down the last few seconds. "Ten! . . . nine! . . . eight! . . ."

A sense of drama and great emotion swept over me, and I felt a strong urge to say something memorable and important. But all I could think of was, "Okay, men, this is it!" And so I decided, wisely, to say nothing at all.

"Three . . . two . . . one . . . *retro!*" cried the retro officer. And at that instant the rocket flashed and roared to life, spewing a long plume of pale yellow flame. At the instant of ignition, the rocket exhibited the now-familiar sudden thrust buildup that pressed us firmly against our couches. The spaceship held rock-steady throughout the twelve-second firing and all our meters looked reassuringly normal.

At cutoff, the rocket shut down as abruptly as it had started. The ship had slowed just enough to begin falling gradually, ever so slowly, toward the earth.

In the twelve-second interval, the engine had slowed our orbital velocity by two hundred miles an hour, just enough to put us on a gradual descent, and if all went well, a safe landing in the Atlantic Ocean thirty minutes later. That main rocket—old reliable—worked perfectly for the eighth and final time, and we were on our way home!

10. Splashdown

No sooner had the thrusting stopped than we took over manual control. Wally started maneuvering us toward the attitude for separating the Service Module, the cylinder-shaped aft section of the spacecraft that had carried propellants, rocket engines, fuel cells and reactants, and life-giving oxygen for eleven days in space. Since it was no longer needed, the module would be cut loose to make its own descent into the atmosphere. After splendidly supporting us all those days, the Service Module would suffer the fiery fate of burning to cinders during its own separate descent through the atmosphere. Heat from the friction and pressure that would build up from its speed through the air would burn and melt the large tin can to cinders and vapor, long before it could reach ground level. Condemning it to this violent demise seemed a harsh reward for such fine service. Harsh, but necessary, for we could not make our own safe entry with the service module attached. It had no heat protective surface of its own, and it covered our main shield on the base of the conical-shaped command module.

The computer display was showing us our velocity errors, or residuals, for the deorbit burn. If the errors were too large, we could have to null them out with our small reaction rockets, or retarget the computer's entry program to compensate.

"Look at that, guys!" I exclaimed. "Damn near perfect!" And they were: one foot per second error along the line of thrust, considerably less in the lateral direction. There would be no need for nulling.

"Beautiful!" Wally shouted.

"Looks like we got a good one; that's the best burn yet!" added Walt with enthusiasm.

"Houston, how do we look?" queried Wally.

"Good burn, *Apollo 7*. We got your residuals. Don't bother nulling."

"Roger, how's our trajectory?"

"You're looking good for entry, Seven. Right on the money. Looks like you won't need an entry update. We'll verify that in a few minutes."

"Roger, Houston."

We were still in space. We wouldn't splash down for another thirty minutes or so. We'd hit the atmosphere in a few minutes and the forces would build up just like they did during launch. It was not a time to be loose in the cabin.

After a few minutes' silence, the capcom called again. "*Apollo 7*, we confirm, your entry data is good. No, repeat, no update required. Use what you've got. And also, you're 'go' for separation."

"Roger, understand no update and we're go for sm sep."

Walt announced, "Thirty seconds to separation. Everybody ready?"

"We're all set," I said, my eyes scanning the instrument panel.

"Okay . . . standby . . . ready . . . *separate!*" Walt called out.

We got the controls set for separation and at the proper time I threw the switches marked "sm sep." A loud, sharp *CRACK!* and a small vibration resounded though the ship and told us that the ring-shaped explosive charge had blown, and the Service Module had departed. The Service Module backed away slowly and began a slow roll as its small rocket jets fired automatically.

We got another surprise. The red master warning lights lit up, and a loud buzzer alarm warbled in our headsets. Two yellow lights illuminated to inform us we had low voltage on both main busses.

"Oh! Oh!" cried Wally. "We've got a problem."

Some yellow lights also came on that read "Main Bus Lo Volts."

"Hey Walt, what the hell is going on?" Wally demanded.

In a flash, Walt checked his voltmeters. "Twenty-one volts," he announced. "We should have twenty-eight."

"Twenty-four volts—both busses!" he shot back.

"Oh Christ, there goes the computer," I complained with disgust and alarm. Our electronic abacus was guaranteed to operate on line voltage between twenty-six and thirty-one volts. At twenty-four, all bets were off.

"Why?" asked Wally.

"It's not guaranteed to work at less than twenty-six volts. I hope you're ready to fly this thing down yourself."

"Sob!" Wally moaned.

"Sorry about that," Walt quipped. "Guess the charges didn't do so hot after all."

"You'll be sorry, all right," I retorted. "We may have to fly this son of a bitch home by hand. Hope you're prepared for a long quiet time on the water while they come looking for us."

We'd had trouble with the battery chargers earlier in the flight, but the batteries themselves had always checked out good. Evidently the sudden drain of the ship's full electrical load, when we gave up the fuel cells at separation, was too much. As the Service Module separated we went on to battery power, and our low voltage warning light came on.

"*Apollo 7*, Houston. We're reading low bus voltage on the downlink," advised the capcom.

No crap, I thought. What gave you the first clue?

"Roger, Houston. Check our computer," I insisted. The lights went out, and Walt announced we had twenty-six and a half volts. Evidently we had experienced only a momentary surge.

"The computer looks good, Donn, but we'll double-check," answered the capcom.

"I wish you would," Wally said. "I don't want to blow this thing on a bad computer."

After a short pause capcom called again. "Okay, Wally, the computer checks out fine. You're still go for automatic."

"Rodge. Thanks for the good news," cracked Wally. We didn't lose the computer. It kept on running, doing its thing for entry. That spacecraft was a winner.

About one minute after separation, I glanced out the hatch window at the Service Module, about half a mile behind us. Its thrusters were burning, and as it spun around the exhaust plume pattern from its roll jets looked like a bright orange-pink pinwheel. We were maneuvering, and I only saw the Service Module a few seconds. But that was enough to reassure us we were well clear and would have no risk of colliding with the ponderous tin can. A few seconds later the spacecraft rolled and the Service Module disappeared.

Wally maneuvered to entry attitude. Several minutes remained until we hit the atmosphere. Walt and I took turns flying the ship on the Command Module control system. The spacecraft responded nicely, and we all felt comfortable about flying manual entry if we had to.

From the crew's point of view, the spacecraft begins reentry in the peculiar posture of upside down and backward—or heads down and blunt end forward, as they say in space parlance. The ship is cocked so that the small end points upward about twenty degrees. The earth's horizon cannot be seen through the forward viewing windows, but it does intersect the center crewman's view through the hatch window. Thus the round viewing window in the hatch can serve as a last-ditch backup attitude reference in the unlikely event of some massive malfunction that would wipe out the computer and all the flight control displays in the cockpit.

During its descent through the atmosphere, the spacecraft develops a lifting force. The entry flight path is controlled by the direction of lift: up, down, left, and right. To control the direction of lift, the ship rolls to different angles throughout entry. With computer guidance the roll angle changes continually to bring the ship down at the intended landing point. For manually controlled entry without guidance, one holds a constant angle of bank—usually sixty degrees from "wings level" (if there were any wings)—and hopes for the best. Since the inverted, backward-looking view through the hatch window is difficult to interpret, on *Apollo 7* we had reference marks etched on the glass for wings—level and sixty degrees of bank.

A light came on telling us we had entered the high, thin edge of the atmosphere and were starting to slow down. The spaceship began to roll and turn as the computer steered it toward the landing target, still several hundred miles away. The rolling motion felt something like a carnival ride. "This reminds me of the Teacup Ride at Disneyland," I observed.

Entry guidance started as we hit the upper fringe of the atmosphere. As we descended through seventy miles' altitude, we began to feel the decelerative force of air drag at our backs. Through our windows we could see the bright hues of a trail of ionized gas caused by the intense heat of entry. It was a light pastel pink, like sherbet. We could see the swirling corkscrew trail of glowing air forming behind us: a fiery pathway that changed color from pink to lavender to purple to orange as we descended. Now and then small flakes of material would peel off the heat shield with a loud pop and dance crazily past the ship's windows in a bright orange shower of sparkles.

The thin air rushing past gave a faint hissing sound. The hissing grew to a low whining whistle, and then to a muffled roar as the air thickened and the pressure built up. The heat shield temperature was several thousand degrees, a mere few inches away. Our cabin temperature held steady at a comfortable eighty degrees, and felt cool as ever. The drag force increased steadily to three times gravity and held at that level most of the way down, mashing us once again hard against the backs of our couches. I could feel the g-force building up—it felt like more than three g's after being weightless for eleven days. Roll maneuvers gave a carnival-ride quality to the ship's motion, but otherwise our ride home to Earth was smooth and stable.

The g-force felt less and less now as we descended. As our velocity slowed, the glowing gases disappeared, the heat shield stopped popping, and the g-force reduced to that of normal gravity. The flight path got steeper until at about fifty thousand feet we were going straight down. Out the windows the blackness of space turned to deep blue sky, then gray as we went through clouds. Fifty thousand feet, forty thousand, thirty thousand—the parachutes should come out now. The small drogue chutes should pop out automatically at twenty-four thousand feet, the three large main chutes at ten thousand. I was ready to mash the parachute button in case the automatic system didn't work. But I didn't have to.

At twenty-four thousand feet, mortar charges expelled the drogue parachutes out of stubby round tubes on the outside top deck of the spacecraft. I expected a big jolt when the drogues opened, but we could hardly feel it. I couldn't see the chutes, but Walt and Wally could. They assured me the drogues were in fine shape. There were some mild oscillations of the ship that soon damped out. At eleven thousand feet, the main chutes deployed, streamed out, and unfurled gracefully into three big, beautiful orange-and-white nylon blossoms. "Now there is truly one of the great, lovely sights of all time," said Walt, for he and Wally could see the chutes blossoming directly above them through their viewing windows.

With the chutes opened so perfectly, a safe landing was almost certain. The three of us felt a noticeable relaxing of tension. The main parachutes operate as a single system, and there isn't any backup. The chances of their failing to open is remote, and actually any two of the three will do, but nevertheless one does tend to worry a little until they deploy. The parachute system was designed to accommodate a spacecraft weight of eleven thousand pounds. Ours was two thousand pounds heavier on account of the heavy hatch and other design changes incorporated as a result of the *Apollo 1* fire, and our safety margins on the parachutes had suffered accordingly.

As we hung there on three good chutes, I recalled the palaver and the rationalization we had gotten from the sweet-talking parachute engineers on why it was all right to fly with a 7 percent safety margin on parachutes that had been in storage for a year. Military pilots' personal chutes are repacked every sixty days. "After all," they said, "the army and air force use cargo parachutes two years after they are packed."

"Bully for them," we said. "But we're not cargo, and the chutes aren't the same. How many cargo chute failures have there been?"

"Well, ah, none—that we know of. Actually, we don't have that data."

"Well, well. Before you give us any more horseshit about shelf life, how about going out and getting some statistics on chute failures? Meanwhile we'll hold out for six months at the most between chute pack and launch."

Our last weather report before entry had forecast clear skies and calm seas in the landing area, with a slight chance of occasional, widely scattered showers. We entered clouds at thirty thousand feet on the way down. At three thousand feet, still in the soup, we began to suspect that the weather forecast had not been altogether accurate. Not that it mattered much. According to the computer, we were less than a mile from our target point, and we hadn't any control over the landing itself anyway. The recovery helicopters could home in on our radio signals no matter what the weather.

Through the windows the sky appeared dull gray and misty. Raindrops spattered against the glass. Ten, nine, eight thousand . . . Wally watched the altimeter needle unwind and waited for *Apollo 7* to break clear of clouds. Should be soon, I thought.

"Let's call the recovery forces," said Wally.

"Go ahead," Walt advised. "I've already set the antennas."

"Recovery, *Apollo 7*, how do you read, over," Wally called.

After several moments of noisy static a crackly voice broke through. "*Apollo 7*, Recovery 1, you're coming in a little garbled but readable. We've been waiting to hear from you. Can you give us a status report?"

"Everything is fine here," Wally transmitted. "We're all in good shape. We had a nice ride down, courtesy of our computer, and we should be landing right on target. Have you sighted us yet?"

"Negative visual at this time," replied Recovery 1, the lead helicopter from the carrier *Essex*. "We are trying to get a fix on your homing beacon. We are hovering at two hundred feet, just below the overcast. Visibility is less than half a mile, and we are having rain showers."

"Two hundred feet? Half a mile? Rain? What happened to all that good weather we were supposed to have?" I complained to my crewmates.

"I'd say the weather man blew it on his forecast," observed Wally.

"You win some, you lose some," sighed Walt.

A very gentle descent now—we were floating down through the clouds and a little rain shower. Should hit the water anytime now. Our sole remaining concern, really, was the touchdown itself. During our lively heated discourse with Mission Control over the helmet issue, we heard a lot of scare stories about the dire effects of hard landings on bareheaded crewmen. We had been warned to expect a bone-jarring impact. Our heads were well-secured, but waiting for that smack in the back was like waiting for the first swat when the school principal is administering a paddling. The altimeter went through a thousand feet . . . five hundred . . . three hundred . . . zero. Hang on . . . here it comes . . . *thump!* We were still descending and I began to comment on the instrument's inaccuracy when we hit the water.

Splat! Apollo 7 mushed gently onto a large rolling wave of foam and sea water. We were so surprised by the softness of splashdown that we could scarcely believe we had landed. A very soft bump in the back is all we felt. No bone-jarring crunch, no teeth-rattling jolt—a mere gentle smack.

"Was that it?" asked Walt, raising his head and looking across at Wally in wide-eyed astonishment.

"I guess so," said Wally.

"How about that for a softie landing?" I said. "I was all set for a real bash."

"I can't believe it. Are we really down? That was *too* easy!" Walt bubbled.

"Hell, there wasn't anything to it!" I echoed.

"Sob! What was all that talk about hard landings?" added Wally.

Just then, another large wave caught *Apollo 7* at just the right angle and flipped it up on its side. "Look out," cried Wally, "here we go!" Our enthusiasm dampened as the tub-like spacecraft slowly pitched itself upside down and left us hanging helplessly in our shoulder harnesses.

The viewing windows were under water, and through them I could see the parachutes and risers drifting away and sinking slowly through clear pale-green ocean water.

"What a way to end a flight," quipped Wally.

"Four million miles in orbit, and we wind up upside down in the ocean," said Walt.

"It's too bad the NASA administrator won't let us name our spacecraft," I said, smiling. "I've got a great idea for this one."

"What is it?" asked Walt.

"Rub-a-Dub-Dub, Three Men in a Tub," I quipped again.

The cabin grew quiet. We turned off all the pumps, blowers, and inverters to conserve electric power. Our communications antennae were under water. We couldn't talk to anyone, and the recovery planes were milling around in the fog vainly trying to pick up our radio signals.

We began to sweat—literally. Our fresh air vents were immersed, and with the blower off there was no air circulating in the cabin or through our space suits.

The Apollo Command Module was a beautiful ship in flight, but a miserable can on the water. It rolled and tossed and bobbed like a cork, and could float indefinitely upside down—or Stable 2, in laconic engineering jargon.

There was an uprighting system consisting of three inflatable bags that produced enough buoyancy at the top end of the ship to flip it right-side up—or Stable 1. But according to our checklist, we had to wait out a ten-minute cooling-off period after landing before turning on the compressors to fill the bags. If that didn't work we could make an emergency exit through the top hatch, which was now at the bottom, since we were Stable 2, and bob to the surface outside.

There was nothing to do but hang there and jostle around for ten minutes. We made some weak attempts at humor, but they didn't help. The craft's vigorous tossing and the heat and stuffiness made me thoroughly ill.

"Hey fellas," I said faintly, "I hate to tell you this, but I'm afraid I'm going to be sick."

"You look a little green around the gills," Wally said with a sickly grin.

"Oh, God," moaned Walt. "Anybody got a sick sack?"

I produced a plastic bag from my pocket. "How much longer?" I asked apprehensively.

"Four minutes. Hang in there," answered Wally, hoping fervently that I wouldn't throw up and make him or Walt ill as well.

I began to retch, violently and repeatedly. All that came up were gastric juices and the bitter taste of the seasick pill I had swallowed just before entry.

Wally turned on an air compressor that pumped air into three large fiberglass bags on the top deck of the spacecraft. Fully inflated, the bags looked like oversized volleyballs. With agonizing slowness, as the uprighting bags filled with air, the ship began tilting toward right-side up. After an eternity of about five minutes, with one great ponderous heave, the craft righted itself.

"Now we know the Apollo uprighting system really works," commented Walt.

"*Apollo 7, Apollo 7*, this is Rescue 1 calling," an anxious voice grated in our earphones. "If you hear me, please respond."

"Roger, Recovery, *Apollo 7*, we read you loud and clear," Wally called. "Sorry we were out of contact so long. We went upside down, and our antennas were under water."

"Roger, *Apollo 7*, we understand. We're picking up your beacon now, and should be there shortly."

We opened the vent valves and turned on the fans that drew fresh air into the cabin. I sucked in a lungful of fresh cool salt air. After eleven days in that can, that first whiff of glorious earth air smelled sweeter than roses. After fifteen minutes of wretched nausea it even tasted good.

The end of a perfect flight—we're down, we're back, we're safe, we made it, and here come the helicopters. You know something? I wonder if Buck Rogers would believe it!

11. Home

In less than ten minutes we heard the *whap-whap-whapping* of helicopter blades beating the air overhead. Two black-suited swimmers dropped from the helicopter, swam over to the spacecraft, and quickly began attaching a flotation collar around the back of the spacecraft, and a large yellow rubber life raft just below the side hatch to receive us when we climbed out. Through his side window Walt waved to one of the swimmers. The man in the water bobbed up to the window, looked in, and smiled.

We tidied up the cabin, stowed our pressure suits, and donned white Teflon overalls that had been our garb most of the flight. The swimmers jumped onto the life raft and pulled open the hatch on the side of the spacecraft. The sweet, salty aroma of fresh ocean air swept into the cabin. We gratefully inhaled our first breaths of real Earth air in eleven days. A drizzle of rain blowing in through the open hatch felt cool and delicious as it softly pelted on our faces.

We jumped into the yellow rubber raft. Being in the center couch and nearest the hatch, I left the spacecraft first, stepping through the hatch and onto the yellow raft. Two swimmers took me by the arms and helped me as I crawled over the hatch sill.

"Welcome back to Earth, sir," said one of the men.

"Thanks," I replied. "Boy, am I glad to see you fellows. You have really done a great job."

"Thank you, sir," said the swimmer.

Walt and Wally soon appeared in the open hatch and dropped into the life raft with me. The three of us, cold and water-soaked, splashed happily in the water that had collected in the bottom of the raft. It felt marvelously wet and cool, and I had a great urge to jump into the ocean.

Soon another helicopter arrived and lowered a large net. The net, made of nylon mesh stretched over a frame of metal tubes, looked something like a child's playpen hanging by the top edge.

One by one we climbed into the net and were hoisted to the helicopter fifty feet above. Eager hands waited to help us scramble from the net to the flat, safe floor of the helicopter. From the open door through which we had just crawled we took one last view of the small round craft that had been our home for the past eleven days. *Apollo 7* looked strangely out of place on the ocean, bobbing and bouncing like a cork, waves sloshing against its sides and spraying mist over the top. With its three globe-shaped uprighting bags on top and yellow raft alongside, it seemed to be something quite different from the proud, gleaming white ship we had flown into space from Launch Complex 34 at Cape Kennedy.

Recovery 1's engines whined steadily as the craft flew low and fast over the dark-blue, foam-tipped ocean waves. We chatted amiably among ourselves and with the helicopter crewmen. As we neared the carrier, we began to feel butterflies in our stomachs as our thoughts turned toward the things we would be facing over the next few hours.

"Wow! Look at that!" exclaimed Walt, peering out a side window. There below us lay the *Essex* with its crew, all dressed in white, lined up on deck to form great block letters that spelled "APOLLO 7."

"Must be at least a thousand men," I said with awe.

"There it is, men, the United States ship *Essex*. We'll be landing on deck in just a few minutes," spoke Wally in his take-charge voice.

"I sure wish we had razors. I really feel scruffy," I said.

"Listen, with my great looks, nobody is even going to look at you," Walt piped up.

"What do you mean by that?" I huffed indignantly. "With that crazy crewcut and all that loose skin, you look like somebody ran over your head with a lawn mower."

"Come on, you guys, knock it off," Wally demanded sharply. "You're about to join the navy down there, so look sharp." Wally, being an old naval aviator, was looking forward to this triumphant return to the world of aircraft carriers. "Since I'm the commander, I'll get out first. Donn, you follow next. Walt, you bring up the rear."

Within ten minutes, we landed on the deck of the aircraft carrier *Essex*. As the helicopter settled onto the deck, we stared dumbly out the windows at the hundreds of men in formation, a large band of navy musicians, and a broad red carpet that stretched from our landing spot to an elevated platform half the distance to the other end of the deck. As the door swung open, the band began to play "Anchors Aweigh." As we stepped on deck a thousand sailors waved and cheered.

"What a stirring reception," I found myself saying to no one in particular. "I'm overwhelmed. Didn't expect anything like this, did you, Walt?"

"Just keep smiling," said Walt as flashbulbs popped all around.

The chief of the NASA recovery team, a large, balding man of good nature and forceful manner, greeted us and escorted us along a large red carpet to a small platform where we would meet the ship's captain and the admiral of the task force.

We walked along the carpet with an uncertain gait, our legs feeling weak and rubbery after eleven days of weightlessness. I felt light-headed and unsure of my footing. The combined effects of fatigue, weightlessness, and the nausea following our landing showed in my unsteady gait.

We returned salutes and shook hands with sailors, NASA officials, naval officers, and newsmen, as we strolled to the speakers' platform where the admiral in command of the recovery forces waited to greet us. The ship's captain stepped to the microphone. "Welcome aboard, gentlemen, and congratulations!" he shouted with a broad smile across his face. "On behalf of the officers and men of the USS *Essex*, It gives me great pleasure to welcome Captain Wally Schirra, Major Donn Eisele, and Mister Walt Cunningham," he said proudly.

"These gentlemen have just completed the historic first flight of the Apollo spaceship and we salute their achievement. It is a great honor for the *Essex* to be chosen to serve as the recovery ship for this important space mission, and I want to commend all hands for the excellent job you all did in bringing these astronauts safely on board."

A great round of applause arose from the crowd and blew across the deck. Wally walked to the microphone and waited patiently as the clapping and shouting died away. "I can't tell you how pleased Walt, Donn, and I are to be here," he began. "We have had a beautiful flight in a magnificent flying machine called *Apollo 7*. But it's great to be back on this beautiful earth, and feel the deck of the *Essex* firm and solid beneath our feet. Thanks a million to all of you for the outstanding work you have done in recovering the *Apollo 7* spacecraft and its crew."

Another great burst of applause, shouting, and whistling rose up as the band played "The Stars and Stripes Forever." I took the speaker's stand next, followed by Walt. We both did the best we could at finding different words to express the same thoughts as Wally: *Apollo 7* was a great flight but it was truly grand to be back on Earth, on board the *Essex*.

The last to speak was the admiral in command, who talked of pride of the fleet, loyalty, and the great traditions of the naval service. The admiral added his own warm words of welcome for the Apollo crew and stepped down.

"Well, I'm glad that's over," I mumbled to myself. "I wonder what comes next." I didn't have to wait too long to find out, for just then Dr. Jernigan, the chief doctor there from NASA, took me by the elbow and led me a short distance to an elevator. Walt and Wally followed close behind. The elevator delivered us two levels down inside the ship where we entered a long, narrow, dull gray corridor whose walls and floor were made of steel, like the rest of the ship. I listened to the strange hollow ringing of our footsteps.

At the end of the hall we entered a large room filled with tables, benches, large metal lamps on tall stands, test tubes, jars and bottles, and several strange-looking machines. I knew at once that the good times were over, and we must now pay the price. A squad of doctors, nurses, and technicians fell upon us. We were in the eager hands of the postflight medical team.

I was exhausted and my whole body cried for rest. But there was none. We were put to work peeing in bottles and blowing in tubes. For the next several hours we were poked, prodded, thumped, punched, and pierced. Blood samples were drawn at frequent intervals, and although the total amount came to only a few ounces, I felt as if all the blood in my body had been sucked away. A man peered inside our eyeballs with a small lighted instrument, and we were whirled, tilted, and whacked. On a bicycle exercise machine we pedaled until we scarcely had strength to stand when we got off. My capacity to exercise was nil. Merely freewheeling the pedals raised my pulse to 120, and when a small load was applied my heart raced at 180 beats a minute.

A doctor asked me to hop up on an examination table. He put his hand on some pipes about seven feet off the floor so I wouldn't hit my head on them as I climbed up. I misunderstood, thinking he wanted me to float up on to the pipes. It seemed completely normal to me after so many days in space. As soon as I realized I couldn't do that anymore, I felt very frustrated.

"I couldn't believe it when Doc Jernigan said, 'That's all, fellows, you can go now,'" said Walt as we walked to our quarters.

"I'm sure glad it's over," I said as we walked through the door of a small, bright room near the captain's quarters.

"Here we are, gentlemen. I hope you'll be comfortable," said our escort, a cheerful young lieutenant.

"This is fine," said Wally. "Thanks a lot."

I lay across my soft, comfortable bunk. Despite the elation of safe return from space, and the satisfaction of completing an eminently successful mission, I felt strangely deprived at the loss of the weightless condition. I resented the constraints of gravity that held me fast to the deck, and on several occasions I caught myself trying to push off and float, rather than walk, from one place to another. I found gravity very confining. After floating weightless for eleven days, it was disappointing to be stuck fast to the floor again.

After showering and shaving, we put on clean underwear and fresh blue suits of two-piece cotton coveralls. "Boy, that hot shower really felt great," said Wally, inhaling a deep, satisfying breath of air.

"Yeah, it sure beats those sponge baths we took in orbit with no soap," said Walt.

"I tried trimming my beard," I said, "but it looked so dumb I just shaved the whole thing off."

"It will take more than a shave to do anything for your looks," quipped Walt.

"Who did your face lift? Dr. Frankenstein?" I shot back.

We'd started medical tests at 8:00 a.m. Mid-morning, we were treated to steak and eggs. Rather ordinary fare, I'm sure, but to us it was superb cuisine of the highest elegance. Our companions lingered comfortably over coffee. Being a navy man himself, Wally enjoyed talking ships and swapping stories—some of which may even have been true—with the officers. Someday, he secretly hoped, he would command a great vessel like the *Essex* himself. And of course Walt always liked to get his two cents' worth into any conversation.

Then a sailor came in with word that the president was waiting to speak with the astronauts.

"The president?" blurted Walt. "The president of what?"

"The president of the United States, sir," said the sailor. "He is waiting at the White House."

"Imagine that!" I exclaimed. "President Johnson, calling us!"

"Oh, he does that after all the missions," said Wally with a casual toss of his head, letting everyone know that he was an old hand at this space-flight business.

We followed the sailor to the ship's radio room where three telephones had been rigged up just for this occasion. We each picked up a telephone and heard the president speak on the other end of the line. "Wally, Walt, Donn, this is the president, speaking from the White House," Mr. Johnson's great voice rung out. "How are you all feeling?"

"Just fine, sir, thank you," we all replied.

I was terribly impressed and honored to get a personal call from the president. But after a brief exchange of amiable chatter, his words took on a strangely stiff and impersonal quality, as if he was reading a speech—which I'm sure he was, since millions of people were watching and listening. He launched into a formal statement that sounded less like a private talk than it did a public speech.

"I want to wish you all a safe trip home," the president concluded, "and I hope you will come and visit us soon, at the White House or the ranch in Texas."

"Thank you, Mr. President," replied Wally, "we'll do that as soon as we can."

"Thank you kindly, sir," I added. "It was awfully nice of you to call."

"Mr. President," Walt began, "I want to thank you from the bottom of my heart for this great honor you have bestowed on us. Talking with you is the high point of our entire spaceflight experience, and I shall long cherish the memory of this historic occasion."

"Aw, for gosh sakes, Walt, dry up," I rasped hoarsely out of the corner of my mouth.

After the president had hung up, Walt said, "Listen, it isn't every day you get a chance to have a personal conversation with the president of the United States, with millions of people listening in."

"There's no biz like showbiz," agreed Wally. "But who wants to hear that baloney you put out?"

"I always say, if you've got it, flaunt it," cracked Walt.

"Well, maybe," I said.

We also talked with our wives, but the words came oddly distant and casual and masked tender sentiments and intimacies in deference to a sense of an eavesdropping world's presence.

By one o'clock, we had sacrificed the requisite pound of flesh to the medics and were released to have lunch with the admiral and his staff. We entered a large dining hall filled with tables covered with white tablecloths and adorned with pewter candlesticks and fancy china, silverware all polished and shiny, and gleaming, clear crystal goblets.

"Look at that spread!" I exclaimed.

"Remember, this is the navy, fellows," Wally said proudly. "Strictly first class."

Delicious hot soup was served, followed by steak: thick, sizzling slabs of beef, dark brown on the outside, pink and juicy in the middle. There were baked potatoes and no end of salads, cooked vegetables, and breads. For dessert the cook rolled out an enormous cake in the shape of an aircraft carrier, eight feet long and weighing three hundred pounds. Large fancy letters decorated the top with the words "USS ESSEX WELCOMES APOLLO SEVEN." Flashbulbs popped as we cut the first pieces with a sword. Then the cooks took over the cake slicing. There was enough to give a generous portion to every person on the ship, and plenty left over.

The luncheon was a social affair, nicely served in the fine navy tradition by Filipino stewards with linens, silver, and china. The admiral himself was amiable, engaging, and urbane. Our blue coveralls and black tennis shoes contrasted starkly with the sumptuous setting and the officers' sparkling white uniforms, but I suppose we could have come in jockey shorts and it wouldn't have mattered. The men there spoke with pride and enthusiasm on the morning's recovery operations, and having lunch with a returning space crew no doubt was a memorable occasion for them.

Following lunch, the three of us spent two hours alone debriefing ourselves with the aid of a tape recorder. The idea was to record our subjective impressions of the flight while they were still fresh in our minds. In our disorganized, undisciplined discourse, we digressed and rambled at random over dozens of small events and circumstances of the previous eleven days. The substance of this hodgepodge of remarks was of little value technically, but we benefited from the rest and quiet this two-hour respite afforded us.

Supper was a gala to-do in a large dining hall below decks. Pervasive jocularity reflected in the diners' smiles and laughter and in the animated remarks of the numerous after-dinner speakers. Following this sprightly affair, we walked to the hangar deck where throngs of sailors gathered to greet us. The cook gave me a normal-size cake in a box to take home to my small son, Jon, who had starred prominently in the television coverage of my family during the flight.

After an interminable round of hand-shaking and autograph signing, the gathering broke up as the sailors gradually drifted away. I looked forward to a long night's sleep with desperate anticipation. I had been awake for twenty-eight hours, and had slept only three hours the last night in orbit. I had been running on nothing but raw nervous energy most of the day. Everyone on the ship, it seemed, had wanted to see us, touch us, shake hands, or otherwise have some personal contact. Those people on the *Essex* were the most delightfully sincere, openly admiring, and hospitable hosts that one could imagine. I loved them all, but we had endured more "showcase" that day than I could tolerate. The strange surroundings, and the kaleidoscope blur of smiling, unfamiliar faces thrust before me, had created a turn of emotional shock that bordered at times on the schizophrenic.

Despite intense fatigue, we were still euphorically high and welcomed the admiral's invitation to visit quietly with our jovial host in his quarters. Thirty minutes of Cokes, popcorn, and conversation proved an effective relaxant.

"I guess we'd all better get some sleep," I said. "Tomorrow we have to get up early and catch a plane back to Florida."

At ten o'clock we tumbled gratefully into our bunks. I fell asleep instantly. That was a long day for me, and I was pooped. But it had been so much fun. The ship's crew had been so glad to see us. I was just glad to be *somewhere*.

During the night the *Essex* steamed westward at full speed toward the Florida coast. By morning we were within flying distance of Cape Kennedy. When the alarm rang at 6:00 a.m., three sleepy people rolled over and slowly got out of bed. "That seemed like a pretty short night," Walt rumbled as he pulled on his trousers. No one else spoke, for Wally and I were not quite awake enough to talk.

We walked through a door that led to an adjoining compartment that served as the captain's private dining room, where we enjoyed a hearty breakfast of ham and eggs, biscuits, orange juice, and coffee.

"I imagine you fellows will have quite a reception when you reach the mainland," said the captain, who sat across the small round table from Wally.

"We're going to have a whole string of receptions, interviews, and meetings," Wally replied, swallowing a bite of biscuit. "Frankly, I would rather skip most of them."

"Don't worry about it, Wally," advised Walt flippantly. "Just relax. I'll take care of everything."

"That's what I'm afraid of," Wally shot back.

"We'll only be famous for a little while," said Walt. "Probably just until the next spaceflight takes off. We might as well enjoy it while we can."

"Well, I think we owe a lot to all those people who helped put us up there in orbit," I asserted. "The least we can do is share our experiences with them."

We ate quickly, then stepped back to our cabin to pick up a few belongings. We bid hasty farewells to our hosts, strode from the cabin, and headed for the ladder that led to the ship's main flight deck. There, three twin-engine utility airplanes, their engines already running, waited to take us and the other NASA people back to Cape Kennedy. Wally, Walt, and I put on bright orange life jackets and boarded the planes, each man to a different aircraft since we had been asked to help fly back to Florida.

I settled into the copilot's seat. The aircraft carrier's catapult shot us into the air, pushing me briefly against the back of my seat, much as the main rocket on *Apollo 7* had done. The plane swooped low out over water— shining blue as sapphires in the bright morning sun.

Two hours' flight across blue water brought us to the landing strip at the Kennedy launch center. The planes touched down and rolled to a stop. Several automobiles arrived to transport us and the others to the other end of the airfield where a large gathering of people milled about. As the cars pulled up near the crowd, several men began running back and forth, shouting and waving their arms with great energy. We stood up and walked across the sun-baked asphalt surface of the airstrip.

An assembly of fans, friends, and well-wishers greeted our arrival, many of them the same people who had lined the halls and walkways of the operations building the day of our launch. There followed another short ceremony of accolades, applause, and welcoming remarks. Walt, Wally, and I expressed our satisfaction with the *Apollo 7* flight, our pleasure in returning to the Cape, and our gratitude to the assemblage for their warm welcome and fine support of our mission.

12. After the Flight

With minor variations, this same welcoming ritual would be repeated innumerable times over the next several weeks. Everywhere we went—our arrival at Ellington Air Base in Houston, the astronaut offices at Cape Kennedy and the Manned Spacecraft Center, our home neighborhoods, press conferences, parties, receptions, personal appearances, hometown visits—people turned out in droves to meet us, speak with us, present awards, and congratulate us. It was all very heady stuff. The crushing crowds, the celebrants' spontaneous outpouring of acclaim, and the awards and honors pumped up the ego to bursting point. We were Saturday's heroes, and we and the rest of NASA rode the crest of the popularity wave for all it was worth. After two years' dormancy, after the tragic *Apollo 1* fire and its aftermath of breast-beating, hand-wringing, subtle recriminations, and public criticism, the manned space program was off and running again.

After a time the approbations, the hurrahs and hoopla, became burdensome, trite, and stale. I began to dread each event as its appointed time approached. What can you say after you've said a hundred times, thank you, how great it was to fly *Apollo 7*, how wonderful it is to be back?

You know yourself what you accomplished. It's nice when others recognize your achievements, but the way you feel about yourself is more important. It doesn't pay to worry too much about what others think.

Immediately after our flight, Walt and I held high hopes of some real goody materializing—an international goodwill tour, a visit to the Paris Air Show, or some other distinctive event like crews of earlier flights had fallen heir to. There were several reasons, I suppose, why it never happened.

Nineteen sixty-eight was an election year, but President Johnson had chosen not to run again and felt no need or desire for political exploitation of astronauts. After the two-year layoff in spaceflights, the State Department did not immediately react to whatever diplomatic value there may be to return-ing space crews—not until after other, grander flights had superseded and overshadowed our own modest Earth orbit effort. (The most widely heralded and sought-after crews are always the ones from the most recent flights.)

Wally had also made known his own disinterest in appearances and public affairs. After long years in the limelight and experiences following his Mercury and Gemini flights, he was understandably blasé and weary of it all. After ten long years and three space missions, he had decided against seeking any more flight assignments. He had filled all the squares on his achievement chart—indeed, what can any of us do for an encore?—and became preoccupied with thoughts and plans for his future endeavors outside NASA.

Walt, Wally, and I are the only ones who will ever know what the flight of *Apollo 7* was really like. I'll always remember.

Afterword

Susie Eisele Black

After *Apollo 7*, Donn and Harriet divorced. The gossip in Houston and the press created a circus atmosphere, but actually Donn was neck-and-neck with a fellow astronaut over who got the first divorce, with another astronaut coming in a close third. With all the media attention on Donn, it allowed the other two to slip out the back door. And, of course, those three were just the tip of the divorce iceberg.

Donn had been assigned to the backup crew for *Apollo 10*. Did he think it would turn into flying another Apollo mission, this time to the moon? I have no idea; he never mentioned it. I don't think any of the guys ever mentioned it, although maybe they talked among themselves. I knew for myself that it wasn't going to turn into a prime crew when it was clear his divorce was going through: all hell broke loose. I could see the way the other guys were acting toward Donn and that he wasn't going to do anything. I think maybe he thought he could go to work, do what he was supposed to do, keep his head down, and it would blow over. But I also know that there were a few things that most astronauts got to do, and he wasn't invited to do them. That hurt his feelings. It was not a nice time at all. I'm almost sure, had he been able to patch things up with Harriet, he would have flown in space again.

After his work on *Apollo 10*, Donn and I were married on August 1969, in Cocoa Beach, at the Holiday Inn. None of Donn's so-called friends were there. Al Bishop, a very good friend of the astronauts, was there as best man. My friends were there, and people from the community were there. But it wasn't a big crowd—I'd say thirty, at the most. It was on a Saturday, it wasn't in Houston, but the main reason other astronauts did not show was that, at this point, the men were running scared. It was bizarre to me, being an outsider. I couldn't believe people lived like that.

Chief astronaut Deke Slayton had asked me to continue seeing Donn until the *Apollo 7* flight, to support him, which I thought was bizarre. Deke would call me up and ask if the guys could come up to my apartment and have a little party that night. So they'd all come over and do their dancing and drinking and whatever, usually about once every two weeks. Prior to that, I'd never had anything to do with the space program. I didn't work for a contractor, didn't know anything about it. So why didn't they come to our wedding? I always imagined it was because they were pissed off. It was later explained to me that Donn and I had broken an unwritten rule: we were not supposed to fall in love. The astronauts' after-hours pastimes at the Cape were supposed to be just diversions from work. When the flight was over, there was no longer any need for a diversion—it was home to Houston. Since I was never part of the female entourage down at the Cape who had casual flings with astronauts, I didn't know this unwritten rule. It seems that it never occurred to them that you might fall in love with a woman and want to be with her. It took Donn a long time to get over that. Writing his book was probably a catharsis.

I left my home in Cape Canaveral with my daughter, Kristy, to live with Donn in Houston, in time for her to start the first grade at the beginning of the school year. I found Houston very unpleasant, and I was very unhappy. Prior to coming to Houston I'd had a very private life; NASA's communal lifestyle was a shock to me.

I'm often asked about the group that has since been mythologized as the Astronaut Wives Club. When Donn and I were married and I moved down to Houston, astronaut wife Beth Williams, a widow by this point, was desperate for me to go to this get-together of the wives. "I guess," I said—I was going to go. And then another astronaut's girlfriend from the Cape whom I knew, she called me and said her boyfriend had wanted her to call and tell me, if I went, there would be a mass walkout by the other wives. It was going to be ugly. Well, that stopped that; I wasn't there for anything like that. So I told Beth, I said, I'm not going to go—not in the middle of something like that. I mean, what is all *that* about?

I think that some of these women were caught up in all the space program publicity. Before their husbands became astronauts they'd had their little clubs, the Officer's Wives Club or something, at some military base. That was what they were used to. They weren't used to *this*—and they didn't know how to act. So the wives gave their astronaut husbands a hard time about me. I think some of the husbands were also afraid I knew too much about their Cape activities and might spill the beans. Donn and I even went to a therapist. I'll never forget it, the therapist said, "You know, Donn, you two are not paranoid—these people *really* don't like her!"

Marilyn Lovell was one of the few astronaut wives who made the effort to be nice to me. Not to the point where I thought she and her husband were my best friends, or that they called us up to go out to dinner or anything, but she always treated me pleasantly. Jim Lovell and Donn had been classmates at Annapolis together, and I assumed he'd asked her to be nice to me. She was friendly, whereas Jane, astronaut Pete Conrad's wife, wouldn't even look at me. But later on, around 1980, we were all together in Washington DC at an affair hosted by President Reagan. We went to have lunch afterward, and Jane said, "I am sorry that I treated you the way I did. Pete told me I shouldn't talk to you." I was just stunned that a strong woman like her would allow herself to be told what to do.

It was at this very difficult time for us that Donn started writing, keeping notes on his observations and thoughts on what he called "Space Biz." We had met novelist James Clavell at a big function after the premiere of the movie *Marooned*. He was so thrilled to meet an astronaut, and he invited us to lunch the next day. We sat there and talked, and he gave Donn the idea that he ought to write.

In May of 1970 Ed Cortright, the director of NASA's Langley Research Center, asked Donn to come to Virginia and work on some research for the forthcoming *Skylab* space station. Donn said yes, so we moved to Virginia and rented a home in Williamsburg. Donn went up first and checked it out, and then we went up, scouted it out, said yes, rented a house, and we lived in Williamsburg for about a year and half. Donn drove his classic 1948 MG TC automobile to work. We also had a small plane, and we would fly around the East Coast making personal appearances for NASA and for our local congressman.

We made many friends among Donn's colleagues at Langley and in the local area, and our lives became much happier. I still have very good friends from that happy time. In a different environment, without all the baggage, he could be considered a former Apollo astronaut in his own right. And because of Donn's astronaut past, many people wanted to get to know him. When we first moved to Williamsburg, I heard a knock on the door one day and when I opened it there was a small boy, about five years old, asking if my daddy could come out and play. That Christmas, as a joke, I gave Donn a doormat that said "Go Away."

Donn and I were just treated like we belonged there. When Walter Cronkite could not make a party, he would suggest that they call us, so we were invited to magnificent weekends in the capital, at old plantations out on the James River: we used to be written up in those Washington gossip columns. Folks from the local college would invite us to their house for dinner parties with famous authors. It was just a scream to live there.

In June of 1972, Donn resigned from NASA and the air force as a full colonel. We had decided that the Vietnam War was so ugly, and we sort of sided with the generals who thought the war might be ruining the military. Donn wrote to one of his Washington friends, who in turn wrote a letter to President Nixon's chief of staff, saying Donn wanted to be involved in some job out of the country. After discussing which country, the president then appointed him as the country director of the Peace Corps for Thailand. By then we had added another Eisele to the family; our son Andrew was born in February 1972. In July we left Williamsburg to spend two years in Bangkok, when Andrew was only a few months old.

Our life took another path. Keeping tabs on two hundred and seventy-five volunteers was quite a job, and Donn did not have time to write his memoirs for a while. Donn's arrival also created mixed feelings among the people he worked with. Everything gets political, it seems—there were groups of people on the left who felt a military man had no business being in the Peace Corps. Then there were people on the right who didn't think he should be there either. But you know what, we got in country, and it was a life-turning event for the whole family. We just had this incredible experience.

We returned to Williamsburg in July 1974. We didn't know where we'd go next, because we hadn't put our heads together. Donn eventually decided what he wanted to do next in his life, but it took him a long time to figure that one out. In the meantime he worked more on a book about *Apollo 7*. His day-to-day activities were still somewhat overwhelming, however, so he could not sit down and write on a regular basis. At one point I taped a cartoon to his desk that I had found in the *New Yorker*. It was a picture of a man sitting at a desk and a woman standing behind him, and the caption read, "My first husband wrote five thousand words a day, rain or shine." He thought it was funny, and we used it throughout our life when one of us would procrastinate over something.

I don't know why Donn never finished his book. I know he worked on it in Houston, after we were married, then in Williamsburg, but not so much, and a little more in Thailand. He started other work and other projects. At one point, a man from Palm Beach who had once owned an airline asked Donn to help him start another one. Donn commuted to Washington DC for two years, and we made plans to move there. But eventually Donn realized that this very wealthy man was more interested in planning an airline than actually starting one. It was two years wasted that Donn could have used to finish his book.

I think Donn would have expanded his manuscript if he'd had more time. You have to understand, Donn was very bitter about his treatment. Not just with NASA management; the astronauts were *all* bitter with management. Donn was also very bitter at the way certain friends treated him. Some of them had been his classmates before NASA, and friends through thick and thin. But so were their wives. The terrible irony was, some of those who abandoned him had been the biggest rakes of them all.

Thankfully, over the years, Donn picked up his friendship with the "old Houston crowd." We would attend astronaut reunions; there was at least one a year. By now, at least one astronaut each time would show up with a new wife; I was no longer an oddity. We went to France for one reunion, to Las Vegas, and to Richard Nixon's California home. For a number of years, Al Worden hosted a Boys' Club ball in Palm Beach every December. They were fun, as most astronauts have a great sense of humor, but we always returned home to our private life.

In the 1980s Donn made several trips to Japan and forged a business partnership with a man named Yoshi Yaminashi. The last trip he made to Japan was in December of 1987, for the opening of the Tokyo Space Camp. Donn was instrumental in getting that contract for Nippon Steel. It was a large event—and it was on that trip that he died of a heart attack.

I received a call from the U.S. Embassy telling me what had happened. It was very unexpected for me, and I had to arrange to get Donn's remains home. In the end, Yoshi claimed the body, took it to his family temple, and had it cremated. He then brought the ashes to Washington, where I had them laid to rest with full military honors at Arlington National Cemetery.

In going through Donn's personal effects after he died, I found the notes and writings that he had made over the years. This was before people had personal computers, so they were all typed. I also found that he had kept all his space mementos, childhood mementos, plaques, and awards. Some had his name misspelled, some were meaningless to me. He had even kept his tests from elementary school. He was a real pack rat. It was fifty-seven years of a space hero's life, but I didn't know what to do with most of it except put it back in the box.

When the fortieth anniversary of *Apollo 7* was held at the Frontiers of Flight museum in Dallas, Texas, in 2008, there was a wonderful weekend celebration. With the sad passing of Wally Schirra, my dear friend Walt Cunningham was the only crew member left alive to attend. Standing in front of the *Apollo 7* spacecraft, Neil Armstrong gave a wonderful, moving speech. He acknowledged the importance of *Apollo 7*, explaining Wally, Walt, and Donn's special contribution to the moon program. And after forty years, with the NASA administrator presiding over the ceremony, the space agency awarded each of the *Apollo 7* crew the NASA Distinguished Service Medal. I wished that Donn had still been alive to accept it. I accepted the award in his name. "I always considered Wally, Walt, and Donn heroes," I told the assembled press. "After forty years, it is nice to know that NASA does too."

In 2005 NASA wrote me a letter and told me that all of the Apollo astronauts or their widows would be given a moon rock to be placed in a museum or other public institution of their choice. Since Donn and I had spent our last years together in Fort Lauderdale in Florida, I picked the Broward County Main Library. I wanted a venue that was free and open to anyone who was interested in seeing it. The library has done a wonderful job planning programs around the moon rock display and arranging for school children to see it. The facility continually shows a film about the flight of *Apollo 7*; a friend of mine who works there tells me she sees Donn every day as she heads to and from her office.

Another ceremony to honor Donn took place some years earlier, in 1997: the inauguration of Donn into the Astronaut Hall of Fame. My teenage son Andy went with me, and I asked him to take part in the ceremonies too. When they called Donn's name we went onstage and former astronaut Alan Shepard, who was at that time the president of the Astronaut Scholarship Foundation, gave us a plaque. I thanked Alan and the audience and said I was sorry that Donn was not there to receive it personally. But Andy went to the microphone and said, "What took so long?" To say that Donn's children were angry and hurt at their father's flight being ignored would be an understatement. Through all of this, people have always forgotten that it is the kids who suffer, because it is the kids who carry the legacy. I am really so sorry for all of the bitterness they went through. The 2008 event in Dallas did a lot to heal that, and I hope that this book will further give Donn some long-due recognition for his hard work and also share his unique insights on the birth of the moon program.

I think a large part of the reason this book needs to be published is to defend his honor. Do you know how many books that have been written with Donn and me in there, that not one author asked us about when they were writing theirs? There have also been television dramatizations I have watched with my mouth hanging open. One had Donn being with me the night before the launch, so that he was late for his own flight. That's not fair, because it is a lie, and the public will think it's what happened. Donn's sons were watching too. When we got together afterward, they said, "That wasn't *my* dad." I know all of Donn's children will be happy that this book puts straight so many inaccuracies.

I want to thank Francis French, who came up with the idea of trying to make sense of Donn's writings. Francis found Donn a mystery when it came to the history of the space program, and we emailed for many months when he was writing *In the Shadow of the Moon*. When I later invited him to come and stay at my home, I showed him the many boxes of Donn's papers I had been carting around for two decades. He did a brilliant job editing Donn's memoirs, and when he sent the first draft to me and I read it, tears came to my eyes. It was like Donn was speaking from the grave. He's been gone for a quarter of a century, and he probably wrote his drafts thirty-five to forty years ago, off and on. But it was like Donn was talking to me. Ever since, I often think about Donn and our lives together. We had a nice life, a very nice, interesting life.

My thanks too to Amy Shira Teitel, who has told the story of the wider space program to put Donn's words in historical context. Both she and Francis have done all of their writing and editing for free, so that the proceeds of this book can help a good cause. I am touched by and grateful for their selflessness, and so are our children.

I hope you find the book both a fascinating look into the very first Apollo flight and into the unique personality of my much-missed late husband. No matter what people say, they'll never be able to take the legacy of being an Apollo astronaut away from Donn. Never, ever, ever.

Historical Overview

Amy Shira Teitel

Donn Eisele never had the opportunity to finish his memoirs. Given more time, it is possible that he would have added more historical context to his memories. It is certainly important for a reader to know just how groundbreaking that first Apollo mission was; the first manned flight of the spacecraft that would take humans to the moon was part of a wider, grander adventure.

When the National Aeronautics and Space Administration opened for business on October 1, 1958, its unofficial goal was to put an American astronaut into space before the Soviet Union launched a cosmonaut. This national need, born from the sting of having been the second nation to launch a satellite, yielded the Mercury program. The Mercury flights could only put one person at a time into space on brief missions, but this short-term program was only the beginning for NASA. Already in 1959 the agency was starting to shape the spacecraft, for a program later named Apollo, that would someday take astronauts all the way to the moon. Less than a decade later, that spacecraft flew on a mission that is now seldom remembered. *Apollo 7* launched on October 11, 1968, the first manned mission of the Apollo program that proved that the core spacecraft, the Command and Service Module, was up for the challenge of taking Americans to the moon. Without *Apollo 7*, the whole lunar landing program could not have taken place, and at the heart of this mission's story is the story of the Apollo Command Module.

The Apollo program was the realization of a long-held dream of humanity. The idea of sending humans to the moon certainly wasn't new when NASA management began considering the idea in the late 1950s. The roots of a lunar landing mission go back at least to the 1860s, when French novelist Jules Verne wrote a story about three men making the journey in *From the Earth to the Moon*. Verne inspired the early rocket and spaceflight pioneers who took the fantastical story and did the necessary scientific calculations to determine how a real mission might work. But one constant that lingered from Verne's day was the expectation that the spacecraft that went to the moon would land and return to Earth; there would be no multiple vehicles going as part of one mission. It was a style of mission depicted in science fiction stories accompanied by images of tall, silvery rockets on alien landscapes with long ladders allowing intrepid explorers a means to explore new worlds.

But there was a problem with this method. Any spacecraft large enough to carry all the propellant for a mission like this would be too heavy to launch from Earth in the first place without an unfathomably large rocket. This problem didn't escape the notice of NASA engineers planning the agency's future, prompting some creative alternative mission profiles to emerge. One involved launching the lunar spacecraft in pieces and assembling it in Earth orbit before going to the moon. Another had the propellant for the return journey sent to the moon's surface in advance of the crew. Still another involved leaving the propellant for the return trip in lunar orbit so the crew could refuel before coming home. However creative, these missions were far from desirable because they all demanded that two spacecraft somehow link up in space. Surely it made more sense to take everything together, and as the 1950s turned into the 1960s, NASA had time to figure out how to do this.

The lunar landing goal was still in the distant future when the United States was again blindsided by a Soviet space accomplishment. On April 12, 1961, Yuri Gagarin became the first person to orbit the earth. It was clear that the Soviets had bigger rockets and more advanced technology than the Americans. Rather than continue to come in second in the space race, President John Kennedy sought to level the playing field. After NASA management assured him a lunar landing was indeed feasible with adequate funding, the president committed the nation to landing a man on the moon and returning him safely home within the decade. The date was May 25, 1961, giving NASA little more than eight years to make good on the president's promise.

Kennedy's pledge gave NASA the "what," "when," "who," and "where," but not the "how" of the lunar landing mission; the "why" was understood as besting the Soviet Union. The "how" question, properly called the lunar landing mode decision, remained open for discussion as the agency pressed on with Apollo. On November 28, 1961, NASA awarded a contract to North American Aviation to build the Apollo spacecraft, but neither agency nor contractor knew how that spacecraft was going to reach its goal. This was a problem, because different modes required different spacecraft. A vehicle assembled in Earth orbit—a so-called Earth orbit rendezvous mode—couldn't be the same as one launched directly to the moon's surface on a direct ascent mission. Further complicating matters was a third mission mode that emerged in late 1961. Called lunar orbit rendezvous (LOR), this involved landing on the moon with a small, dedicated lunar landing vehicle while the main spacecraft with the heat shield and propellant for the return journey would remain in lunar orbit.

LOR was arguably the most complicated method, involving the docking of two spacecraft a quarter of a million miles from Earth, but the benefit was an overall lighter weight for the mission. As 1962 wore on, LOR continually emerged as the best means to achieving the lunar landing within the decade. On October 11, 1962, NASA announced that Apollo would go to the moon via LOR. The decision dealt a blow to North American. The company had spent the last year developing a spacecraft that now wouldn't be landing on the moon. Instead the glory would go to Grumman Aerospace, the company that had won the contract to build the Lunar Module on November 7. But it would still fall to North American to make sure the two spacecraft—its own Command and Service Modules and Grumman's Lunar Module—could work in harmony.

North American's spacecraft was, like the Mercury spacecraft before it, a blunt-bottomed truncated cone, but this was where the similarities ended. The Apollo Command Module would support three astronauts on a two-week journey in a comfortable shirtsleeves environment. Fixed behind the gumdrop shaped spacecraft would be a Service Module holding the mission's consumables: the main propulsion and smaller reaction control systems as well as the fuel cells that would power the spacecraft and give the crew water. But the LOR decision meant that the spacecraft now had to include a docking system with a hatch to allow the astronauts to pass between the two spacecraft in flight. At the same time, NASA asked for a new design of the spacecraft's main hatch so astronauts could perform spacewalks during the missions. These two changes alone were so significant that North American couldn't easily work them into the spacecraft it had been building for months. Instead, it was tasked with simultaneously building two versions of the same spacecraft, only one of which would be able to complete the lunar missions. Rather than scrap the earlier iteration,

North American came up with a novel solution to put past work to good use: a block concept. The first version of the Command Module would be used for hardware checkout flights and crew training missions in Earth orbit. The lunar-capable Block II would fly the big missions to the moon. NASA was amenable to the idea and signed off on both the block concept and the Command Module layout on January 24, 1964.

In the meantime NASA gained more experience in space with ten manned missions in the two-person Gemini spacecraft, a follow-on from the Mercury program. In the background, the Apollo Command Module came to life. The first Command Modules built were boilerplate models, nonworking spacecraft that mimicked the size and weight distribution of the real thing. Flights A-001, A-002, and A-003 all saw boilerplate Block I spacecraft launched on Little Joe II sounding rockets from the White Sands Missile Range in New Mexico, returning valuable data in the process. On February 26, 1966, SA-201 (short for Saturn-Apollo) saw Block I Spacecraft 009 launch on a Saturn IB rocket. This first Command Module in space was also a test of every aspect of a launch from hardware to rocket staging to electrical subsystems plus all the mission support facilities on the ground at Cape Canaveral. The next flight, SA-202, launched Block I Spacecraft 011 on a flight to test the Saturn rocket's S-IVB upper stage as well as the Command Module's boost protective cover, a shroud designed to protect the spacecraft during launch. Taken together, these unmanned missions gathered a full data set on how the Saturn IB rocket worked, and it was decided that the Apollo Command Module was ready to take astronauts into space. With no need for more testing, Spacecraft 012 was earmarked in early 1966 for the first manned mission. Internally designated as AS-204, the flight was informally known as *Apollo 1*.

Commanded by Mercury and Gemini veteran Gus Grissom alongside America's first spacewalker, Ed White, and rookie Roger Chaffee, *Apollo 1* was exactly the mission North American had envisioned for the Block I spacecraft when it came up with the block concept. The flight was a shakedown cruise, a chance for NASA to test all the spacecraft's systems in the relative safety of Earth orbit. If anything went wrong, the crew could be back on Earth in a matter of hours. Barring any anomalies, the crew would stay up for almost two weeks, putting the new spacecraft through its paces.

As *Apollo 1*'s February 21, 1967, launch date neared, NASA raced against the clock to address the handful of outstanding issues with Spacecraft 012. The crews—both Grissom's prime crew and the backup crew of Wally Schirra, Donn Eisele, and Walt Cunningham—similarly struggled to stay abreast of the constant changes being made to their spacecraft. Even the final tests, which were routine for NASA by this point, were problematic. The troubles continued during the plugs-out test, so called because it tested the spacecraft on its own internal power supply with the vehicle stacked on its rocket on the launch pad. At 6:31 p.m., just minutes after sunset on January 27, Grissom, White, and Chaffee had already endured a test dogged by a smell like sour buttermilk in their oxygen systems and communications delays when it is believed a frayed wire in the cabin sparked. In the pure oxygen environment, the spark quickly turned into an inferno. Test controllers heard the word "fire" over the communications loop, but before anyone nearby could free the crew, the spacecraft's hull ruptured. The pad technicians fought against the flames and acrid smoke, but by the time they managed to open the hatch to free the crew, all three astronauts were dead. They were asphyxiated within seconds when toxic smoke seeped into their oxygen supply.

Within hours, the Apollo 204 review board was up and running with plans to disassemble Spacecraft 012 alongside the identical Spacecraft 014. In the months that followed, technicians found frayed wires and other signs of wear from the constant removal and reinstallation of systems, plus evidence of corrosive leaks in the charred spacecraft. The investigation also revealed the problematic but common practice of disconnecting electrical connections while they were powered. And on the whole, the review board determined there was simply too much flammable material in the spacecraft. Soaking in pure oxygen for hours during the plugs-out test had turned Spacecraft 012 into a bomb. It was, in retrospect, a miracle that no fatalities had occurred during plugs-out tests of the Mercury or Gemini spacecraft.

When the fire investigation wrapped up in March of 1967, it was clear that a lot of changes needed to be made to the Command Module before it could go into space. Foremost was a change in the hatch design. The Block I's hatch was a complicated, inward-opening, tripartite one consisting of a lightweight removable hatch, an outward-opening heat shield hatch, and a third hatch on the boost protective cover. With this design, crew egress took ninety seconds under normal conditions at the end of the mission. But the fire was far from normal. To protect against another such incident, the main hatch would have to change, as would the choice of cabin environment. NASA had originally selected pure oxygen because it was simpler and lighter than a less flammable two-gas system. Now, the agency stipulated that the environment at launch be mixed oxygen and nitrogen, a less flammable combination.

Beyond questions of hardware and procedures, however, the fire called into question NASA's approach to the Apollo program. Previously dismissed questions about the need for Block I flights were revisited. No one would argue against testing a new spacecraft in Earth orbit before going to the moon, but was there really a need to fly any Block I spacecraft when it was so drastically different from the Block II model that would go to the moon? Even with some overlapping hardware and systems, it didn't seem necessary. And so, in the wake of the *Apollo 1* fire, NASA canceled manned Block I flights. All Apollo crews would fly in Block II spacecraft.

Four weeks after the fire, Block II Spacecraft 101 was deemed fit to fly providing changes demanded by the Apollo 204 review board were made. By April it was earmarked as the first spacecraft to carry a crew aloft. The crew assigned to this first flight was *Apollo 1*'s backup crew: Schirra, Eisele, and Cunningham. Apollo was getting back on track, but there was still a lot of work to be done before a Command Module could fly.

It wasn't until the end of 1967 that the required hardware changes had been made to Spacecraft 101, including the new, two-part integrated hatch. The inner and outer hatches were now combined into a single outward-opening unit with the boost protective cover separate but connected. Now, one mechanism inside the cabin opened the hatch in seven seconds. The first integrated hatch was retrofitted into Block I Spacecraft 017 and launched as the payload of the unmanned *Apollo 4* mission on November 9, 1967. *Apollo 5* tested an unmanned Lunar Module in orbit before *Apollo 6* took the final unmanned Command Module on a test flight and completed NASA's necessary data-gathering missions. Everything was ready for *Apollo 7*.

On October 11, 1968, just twenty-one months after losing three of their colleagues, Wally Schirra, Donn Eisele, and Walt Cunningham climbed into their Block II Command Module and launched on a Saturn 1B rocket. Once in orbit, the three astronauts got to work almost immediately. Their flight plan was a busy one with key tasks assigned early on in the mission in case they needed to come home early. Their first task was to safe the spent S-IVB upper stage for a rendezvous and station-keeping exercise.

Mission Controllers vented the remaining liquid hydrogen fuel and liquid oxygen from the tanks to avoid a potential explosion, and the crew then fired their main Service Propulsion System—SPS—to close the distance between them and their target.

This exercise was both a test of the SPS engine and a test for a contingency maneuver for lunar missions. On a typical Apollo flight, the moon-walking astronauts would leave the surface in the Lunar Module's ascent stage, then rendezvous with the Command and Service Module in lunar orbit. The Command and Service Module would be the passive vehicle, but the roles would be reversed in an emergency situation and the Command Module would have to collect the Lunar Module. This was the scenario *Apollo 7* was testing with the S-IVB playing the role of a troubled Lunar Module. It was also a maneuver during which the crew could test a host of other vital systems, namely the Apollo guidance and navigation system and the optical tracking system that served as its backup.

The rendezvous complete, the crew moved on to tracking the S-IVB's progress with their sextant and made another six precision burns with the SPS engine to prove it could fire multiple times on a mission. They ran cold soak tests, stabilizing the spacecraft with one side shadowed from sunlight to see how each Service Module system responded to the frigid space environment. They ran tests to see whether the environmental control system radiator surface coating would degrade during a two-week lunar mission. They took hundreds of photographs, and, much to Schirra's frustration over public relations goals superseding engineering ones, they made America's first-ever live television broadcasts from space.

Apollo 7 stayed aloft for eleven days, splashing down safely in the North Atlantic on October 22, and the post-mission report highlighted only a handful of problems that needed to be addressed before the next flight. Intermittent, slightly garbled communications were chalked up to a network issue rather than a spacecraft problem and were easily fixed. Power problems manifesting as a voltage loss in the fuel cells coincident with automatic operation of the fans that stirred the cryogenic gas tanks were solved by a procedural change; now the astronauts would flip the switch to stir the tanks manually. Control problems from a nonresponsive hand controller were chalked up to sticky hardware. Difficulties with the entry monitor system were dismissed as a flawed unit, not an inherent problem with the technology.

NASA also learned some valuable human lessons from *Apollo 7*, owing in large part to the crew's varying levels of discomfort. Not long after reaching orbit, Schirra reported he was coming down with a head cold, and things only got worse from there. Eisele and Cunningham fell in line behind their commander, whose bad mood was exacerbated by the sleep schedule that had one crewmember awake at all times to monitor the spacecraft. As a result, no one slept well on the flight. A final disagreement with Mission Control had come when Schirra refused to wear his helmet during reentry for fear of a burst eardrum from his cold. It was a worrying move for NASA that ultimately had no ill consequences. The Command Module was safe enough for astronauts to return home without pressure suits.

This handful of issues aside, *Apollo 7* was incredibly successful. It set the bar high for future missions and put NASA back on track for the moon. The next flight, *Apollo 8*, took that momentum and ran with it. Without a Lunar Module ready to fly, NASA made the daring decision to send a crew to the moon with only a slightly modified Command and Service Module. This spacecraft had a single combined forward hatch and foldable couches, two changes necessary for missions where astronauts would be transferring between the Command and Service Module and Lunar Module midflight. The computer program was changed for this mission to one that could navigate between the earth and the moon. *Apollo 8* launched on December 21, 1968, orbited the moon ten times over Christmas, and then returned home for splashdown on December 27.

With two manned Command and Service Module missions under its belt, NASA shifted focus onto the Lunar Module and the docking mechanism that would link the two spacecraft in flight. Testing this last piece of the lunar mission puzzle was *Apollo 9*'s charge, which it did during its ten-day mission launched on March 3, 1969. Then, on May 18, *Apollo 10* launched on a lunar dress rehearsal mission. The crew went through a full lunar landing mission save the actual landing on the moon, proving the Apollo spacecraft hardware was up to the task. Donn Eisele served on the backup crew, ready to step in if a prime crew member fell ill before launch. The years of design, work, training, and testing came together two months later when, on July 20, *Apollo 11* landed on the moon. The crew splashed down in the Pacific Ocean four days later in the same type of Block II Command Module that *Apollo 7* had tested less than a year earlier.

The Command Module proved itself a workhorse for the remainder of the Apollo program, and it was tasked with an unexpected challenge during *Apollo 13*. On this third lunar landing attempt, one of the Service Module's oxygen tanks exploded, crippling the Command Module and forcing the crew to rely on the Lunar Module for consumables until their trajectory brought them home. But they still needed the Command Module to reenter the atmosphere and splash down, and though it wasn't designed to be shut down and powered up in flight, NASA successfully did just that. Engineers found a way to conserve the Command Module's batteries for the final phase of the mission, powering it up without damaging the vital systems. The crew of *Apollo 13* splashed down safely on April 17, 1970.

But the Apollo program was doomed long before *Apollo 13*'s near disaster. Already in August 1967, it was clear NASA's impressive Apollo-era funding couldn't last. The budget for space exploration was starting to shrink, forcing cancellation of the final three lunar missions and leaving the space agency with excess hardware. The Lunar Module couldn't do anything except land on the moon, but the Command and Service Module could be used for other missions with other goals. So while *Apollos 14, 15, 16*, and *17* flew four successful lunar landing missions, NASA developed a space station concept using the otherwise purposeless Apollo Command Module as the main crew transport vehicle.

The *Skylab* space station was made from an unused S IVB stage and launched on the last Saturn V rocket on May 14, 1973. It was severely damaged during launch and would have been unusable if fast, emergency repairs had not been made. The first crew followed eleven days later, living in the Apollo Command Module during their initial repair duties before successfully moving into the space station for twenty-eight days. Two more *Skylab* crews followed in turn, each one launching and splashing down in a repurposed Apollo Command Module. A final flight of the Apollo spacecraft came in 1975. The American half of the Apollo-Soyuz Test Project, a joint mission with the Soviet Union that symbolically marked the end of the space race, was the last Apollo Command Module to fly.

The Apollo Command Module was retired after the Apollo-Soyuz mission, though its legacy lives on. It remains NASA's most iconic spacecraft even for a generation too young to have seen the moon landings. The spacecraft didn't just take Americans to the moon and ensure they returned safely to Earth:

it delivered astronauts to America's first space station and facilitated history's first international cooperative space mission. And though NASA departed from the blunt body concept in favor of the aircraft-inspired Space Shuttle, NASA retired that vehicle in 2011 and returned to an Apollo-era design with the Orion spacecraft shape. Commercial partners, too, are largely leaning toward a similar blunt-bodied spacecraft. It is, at this point, a tried-and-true design. Over the course of more than a dozen Apollo missions, eleven of which were manned, NASA gained confidence in the style of spacecraft, and concept studies for variations, including a five-person version and another that could support manned missions to Venus and Mars, suggested that it could do far more than fly to the moon and back had it been given the chance.

Much in the way the Command Module is central to Apollo's story, *Apollo 7*'s mission is central to the story of the Command Module. The mission that shakes out a new spacecraft is vital, but often overlooked. *Apollo 7*'s engineering checkout flight might be, for the average person, far less exciting than the missions that came after, the voyages that took that spacecraft to the moon. But none of the later Apollo missions could have flown without *Apollo 7*. To land on the moon, NASA first needed to test the Command and Service and Lunar Modules in lunar orbit. Before these spacecraft could go to the moon at all, the agency needed to test them closer to home, in the relative safety of Earth orbit. And before the Lunar Module could fly, NASA needed to ensure that its core spacecraft, the one that would keep the crew alive throughout a lunar mission and bring them home safely, was good enough for its mission. Donn Eisele's ride into space, the *Apollo 7* flight, was the mission that started it all. We are fortunate to have his engrossing, and very human, firsthand account to tell us, beyond the technical and engineering details, what it was actually *like* to fly that very first mission.

Sources

"Apollo 1 Spacecraft History." NASA. http://history.nasa.gov/SP-4029/Apollo_01b
　　_Spacecraft_History.htm. Accessed January 18, 2014.
"Apollo 7 Air-to-Ground Voice Transcriptions." NASA, Washington DC.
"Apollo 7 Mission Report." NASA, Manned Spacecraft Center, Houston. December 1968.

"Apollo 7 Onboard Voice Transcription." NASA, Manned Spacecraft Center, Houston. December 1968.

"Apollo Operations Handbook, Block II Spacecraft. Volume I Spacecraft Description." NASA, Spacecraft Systems Operation Branch, Flight Crew Support Division. April 15, 1969; changed October 15, 1969.

"Apollo Operations Handbook, Command and Service Module Spacecraft 012." North American Aviation, Inc., Space and Information Systems Division. September 16, 1966.

"Apollo Program Summary Report." NASA, Lyndon B. Johnson Space Center, Houston. April 1975.

"Apollo-Soyuz Test Project Information for Press." NASA, Washington DC. 1975.

Brooks, Courtney G., and Ivan D. Ertel. *The Apollo Spacecraft: A Chronology, Volume 3, October 1, 1964–January 20, 1966*. NASA Historical Series. Washington DC. 1976.

Ertel, Ivan D., and Mary Louise Morse. *The Apollo Spacecraft: A Chronology, Volume 1, Through November 7, 1962*. NASA Historical Series. Washington DC. 1969.

Ertel, Ivan D., and Roland W. Newkirk. With Courtney G. Brooks. *The Apollo Spacecraft: A Chronology, Volume 4, January 21, 1966–July 13, 1974*. NASA Historical Series. Washington DC. 1978.

"Info Sheet: Apollo Hatch Redesign, a Matter of Urgency." Historic Space Systems. December 1996.

Logsdon, John M. *The Decision to Go to the Moon*. Chicago: University of Chicago Press, 1970.

Morse, Mary Louise, and Jean Kernahan Bays. *The Apollo Spacecraft: A Chronology, Volume 2, November 8, 1962–September 30, 1964*. NASA Historical Series. Washington DC. 1973.

"Preliminary Flight Plan Apollo 7." NASA, Manned Spacecraft Center, Houston. May 31, 1968.

"Project: Apollo 7 Press Kit." NASA, Washington DC. October 6, 1968.

"Rendezvous Procedures Apollo 7 (Final Revision A)." NASA, Manned Spacecraft Center, Houston. September 27, 1968.

"Report of Apollo 204 Review Board to the Administrator, National Aeronautics and Space Administration." NASA Historical Reference Collection. Washington DC. April 5, 1967.

"The Skylab Program." NASA, Washington DC. http://history.nasa.gov/apollo/skylab.html. Accessed February 22, 2014.

Stubbs, Sandy M. "Landing Characteristics of the Apollo Spacecraft with Deployed-Heat-Shield Impact Attenuation Systems." Technical Note D-3059. Langley Research Center, Virginia. NASA, Washington DC. January 1966.

Woods, W. David. *How Apollo Flew to the Moon*. Chichester: Springer Praxis, 2008.

Acknowledgments

This book has taken a long journey from the back of a closet to printed form. We wish to thank the many people, named and unnamed, who agreed to read the entire book and make very helpful suggestions. Our thanks to Geoffrey Bowman, Jennifer Brisco, Colin Burgess, Emily Carney, Michael Cassutt, John Charles, Jay Gallentine, David Hitt, Richard Jurek, Bruce Moody, Anne Morrell, Gordon Permann, Robert Reeves, Erin Rogers, David Shomper, Mark Ulett, and Amjad Zaidi for their assistance. Thanks to Rob Taylor, Courtney Ochsner, Sara Springsteen, Tish Fobben, and the entire UNP team for seeing the potential of this book. Colleen Romick Clark did masterful copyediting work on the text. J. L. Pickering of Retro Space Images kindly provided the wonderful NASA images in the book.

My good friend Susie Eisele Black was determined to see Donn's words in print, and she was delighted that it was going to happen. This book is dedicated to her.

Index

In the Outward Odyssey: A People's History of Spaceflight series

To order or obtain more information on these or other University of Nebraska Press titles, visit nebraskapress.unl.edu.